READERS' T

"I keep coming back to this book, mesmerized by the images it conjures up in my mind, and finding in it the unspoken reasons for my rediscovered love of the ocean."—A reader, Nanaimo, British Columbia, Canada

———— ♦♦ ————

"On one level, it is a series of entertaining fishing stories. On another level, it is a view of nature through the eyes of a hunter....I keep a copy of this book on my nightstand and read from it at least three times a month. I can open it up to any page and escape the worries of the day. It is especially nice to read when work keeps me from the ocean for long weeks at a time."—A reader, Long Beach, California

———— ♦♦ ————

"This book will help you realize...what's really important in life. Keep it because you'll want to reread it."—Eric Howard, Kansas City, Missouri

———— ♦♦ ————

"A heart and soul grabber. All true spearos will understand."—L. Bingham, Brooklyn, New York

———— ♦♦ ————

"...truly expresses the true essence of being in the magical aquatic world. This book is masterfully written and it was a real joy to read."—A reader, Torrance, California

LAST OF THE
blue water
HUNTERS

CARLOS EYLES

AQUA QUEST PUBLICATIONS, INC. ■ NEW YORK

Library of Congress Cataloging-in-Publication Data

Eyles, Carlos.
    Last of the blue water hunters / by Carlos Eyles.
        p. cm.
    ISBN 10: 1-881652-33-5 ISBN 13: 978-1-881652-33-5 (pbk.)
    1. Eyles, Carlos. 2. Skin Divers—United States—Biography.
    3. Fishers—United States—Biography. 4. Spear fishing—Pacific
    Coast (North America) I. Title.

GV838.E95A32004
797.23'092—dc22

                                                      2003017270

All photographs, including the cover, are by the author unless otherwise
stated.

First Printing 1985
Cover design: DE Smith, brandingscience.com

Printed in the United States of America
10 9 8 7 6 5 4 3 2

DEDICATION

To Joe Schuch

In researching the history of the Fathers and the Second Generation, scores of names appeared of those who made significant contributions to the evolution of blue water hunting. If I were to try to record every name involved, I would invariably leave some off the list. So I make no list at all, and stay with those with whom I have had direct experience, letting them represent the tribe as a whole. To those blue water hunters, both past and present, not mentioned, yet whose contributions are no less significant, this book is silently dedicated.

ACKNOWLEDGEMENTS

Especially I wish to thank Ernie Dageford: without the unconditional generosity of his gift, the *Infinity*, it is unlikely that this book would have ever set sail. Editor Nancy Roth provided her usual steadfast and inspiring support. For her friendship and clear eye I am everlastingly grateful. Warm thanks are also due to Edward Montague for his critique and constructive suggestions in the final drafts. For their photographic contributions I wish to thank Lamar Boren, George Kuznecovs, Omar Nielson, Frank Rodecker, Bill Brown, Jim Christenson, Jay Riffe, and Howard Benedict.

FOREWORD

It's not an overstatement to say this book changed my life. Back in the mid-1980's, in a time before you could type in "spearfishing" or "free diving" into a web browser and get several hundred pages of information at your fingertips, I was holding my breath while shooting rockfish and collecting abalone in the sleepy backwater of Northern California. Wallowing in dark, cold water, I was clueless to the possibilities that a single breath might offer. Then I found this book in a small dive shop, buried among "how to" SCUBA books and travel logs.

In its pages I found experiences beyond my imagination, discovering a tribe populated by men of skill and courage, who stalked huge fish and were, in turn, stalked themselves. Reading it set me on a path I follow to this day, spear in hand, hovering above an expanse of endless blue.

Today the clan survives, drawn to the experience Carlos describes so well, and is, in fact, growing in numbers. Its continued existence rests on the Ocean's ability to survive the onslaught from the rapacious terrestrial homo sapiens. If there comes a day when there is a "last" member of our tribe, then mankind will have failed to head the warning implicit in this book.

Last of the Blue Water Hunters remains unique in its perspective among today's writings, a soulful and sublime rendering of man merged with the sea. I have little doubt that divers new to this book will continue to find in its pages, their own epiphanies.

Kurt R. Bickel
Senior Editor, Spearfishing Magazine

CONTENTS

PROLOGUE

One September, three years to the month that Terry Maas performed the incredible feat of spearing and landing, single-handed, a three hundred and ninety-eight-pound blue fin tuna, Harry Ingram was diving those same Mexican waters off of the Guadalupe islands, hunting the same fish.

Soon after Terry had bridged that interminable chasm that lies between the impossible and the possible, charter boats loaded with tuna rigs and the best spearfishermen around began to regularly make the two hundred-mile trip down to Guadalupe in search of the ultimate fish.

It was late afternoon, and the water was dirty, thirty to forty feet of visibility, which by any other standard is decent water, but here in these normally crystal clear waters where the visibility exceeds a hundred feet, it was considered poor. Tom Blanford took his short gun into the water in search of a yellowtail for dinner. In almost no time he strung a large blue fin, close to a hundred pounds. Without the flotation that a tuna rig provides he had no chance at the fish, and those in the boat saw him plowing across the water for some seventy feet before the five hundred-pound test line broke, or was severed.

"Tuna," he yelled. And Harry and two other divers suited up while Tom returned to get his tuna rig. Within twenty minutes, Tom had speared another tuna, this one smaller, maybe sixty pounds. The blue fin tore off like a runaway freight train when struck by the spear. Tom returned to the surface and watched the line zip out from his double floated rig. Suddenly the tension relaxed and the line slacked. He gave it a pull, testing the fish, but there was nothing on the other end. Apparently the tuna had pulled out. Not unusual, the soft flesh of the fish combined with its tremendous power make it the most difficult of all fish in the ocean to land. In fact, the stalking techniques for hunting the tuna are still so relatively new that the unknowns outnumber the knowns. Only a few of these fish have been landed. It seems to take the perfect or near perfect placement of an arrow to bring one in. Reluctantly, Tom drew in his line while swimming in the direction the tuna had been heading. Sixty feet from the point of his initial contact with the fish, a ball of blood six feet in diameter hung in the water, far too much blood for the wound of a spear to produce. Odd, thought Tom, I wonder what happened?

He continued to pull in his shooting line and re-string his speargun. Harry had drifted away and was fifty feet or so outside of Tom. Knowing that tuna had moved into the area lifted Harry to that level of ultra-alertness that is generated when a hunter is aware that big game is on the move. He was looking intently in all directions beneath him when he saw the shark.

"It came from behind me and on the right. It was turned slightly on its right side and from twenty feet down looked straight up at me with its left eye. My first thought when I saw its massive girth was, 'I am a dead man.' There was no doubt that it was a great white shark. Later we figured that by its length, somewhere between fifteen and twenty feet, it must have weighed well over three thousand pounds. But at the time none of that registered in me. I lifted my head out of the water and yelled 'Shark,' because I wanted the others to know what had killed me. I've been diving blue water for eight years, and I've seen sharks, but the sight of this enormous creature completely unnerved me. Then it swam about fifty feet away and I thought, maybe I have a chance, maybe it will circle. As the thought cleared my head the shark turned and headed right for me. It covered the fifty feet and was on top of me with its mouth open in half a second."

Several divers on the boat had heard Harry's shark cry, and could see him floating on the surface. Then they saw Harry suddenly thrust backward, lifted waist high and spun out of the water. Ten feet of the expansive back of the shark erupted out of the water (they never saw the head or tail) just in front of him and they saw Harry fall across it in a cascade of thrashing white water. It was as shocking a sight as any blue water hunter could see; but for circumstance it could have been anyone in the boat. To all who witnessed the assault, it was assumed that Harry had been bitten in half. There was no way he could have survived the attack.

In a last act of desperation Harry pulled the trigger on his speargun just before the shark hit him. He doesn't remember the next few moments. Apparently, the shark took the fired arrow plus four feet of spear stock, the last foot of spear stock perhaps being all that stood between Harry and the mouth of the great white. Miraculously, he was not bitten. The force of the shark's momentum drove the butt of the speargun into his left shoulder, spun and lifted him just out of reach of the jaws. As the shark broke water, he fell across the great white's head and rolled over its left eye. Then they both slipped back into the water. The shark turned and struck for the open ocean, dragging the tuna rig and leaving Harry unscathed save for a deep bruise on his left shoulder.

Harry would have been the third fatality as the result of a shark attack on a blue water hunter in Guadalupe waters. A land-bound observer, or the casual recreational diver for that matter, would, with reasonable justification, question why anyone would voluntarily enter such waters knowing their history, particularly if those who enter the water do so without the aid of SCUBA, or the safety of a shark cage, or the protection of a bang stick, whose only defense is the underwater equivalent to the bow and arrow. What motivates a man to such a degree that he is willing to drop his vulnerable self into one of the wildest, most prehistoric territories on the planet? Indeed, why is he drawn to such a wilderness, and how did he find his way into those waters in the first place?

To such questions there can never be complete answers, for the motives of such men are never fully understood, even by themselves. Yet the questions beg for answers, and the answers, at least in part, make for one hell of a story.

1

IN THE BELLY
OF THE MOTHER

The forty-foot Mariner ketch *Infinity* slowly maneuvers her bulk around the last gangway of the Dana Point Marina and noses her bowsprit out into the jetty, impaling as she goes the full moon which has risen large and luminous out of the low hills in the east and begun its ascent into the clear June night. We are bound for the island of Catalina, which lies forty miles northwest of the marina.

Ernie Dageford, owner and skipper of the *Infinity*, has been working long hours, so I take the first watch and he goes below to sleep. It is 10:55 PM as we clear the harbor. I steer a compass heading of 255; we are without sails and the Perkins is running at 1700 rpm. Under these light seas, we should get to the island near daybreak.

Motoring into the crisp moonlight night I think of other crossings, but can't begin to remember them all or even know how many I have made.

The past few years have seen them dwindle to one and two a year from an average of twenty or more a year for a span of thirteen years. The last trip was in the spring a year ago; four of us were diving on the west end of the island, and we came across some yellowtail. (The moon casts itself across the water and breaks into ten thousand smaller moons all dancing on the short chopped sea.) My thoughts mingle with the moon and the fish is before me, big, like a torpedo, moving easily through the thick atmosphere.

I was fortunate to be of a generation that existed for a moment in man's history when that yellowtail could be seen in the wild at eye level, a millisecond in evolutionary time when he first penetrated the surface of a fertile ocean that had yet to be ravaged and laid barren at the hands of civilization.

My kinship with the ocean began on the island of Oahu in the Hawaiian chain. In my first five years I roamed her shores and played in her surf. When I was six I entered her belly and made friends with the creatures that lived there. My heroes were the Hawaiians, who would swim out from shore barefoot, without goggles, and dive into the temperate clear water, returning with mysterious ocean objects and sea creatures that had long lain hidden from the eye of man.

One afternoon the Hawaiians returned from the deep water with a catch that was so impressive it placed me on a path to the underwater world from which I've sometimes strayed but have always managed to return to.

I was playing on the beach when a commotion drew me down to the shoreline. Reaching the water's edge, I watched three young Hawaiians lift an enormous sea turtle out of the surf and on to the beach. It must have weighed several hundred pounds because the men had to struggle with it to bring it farther up onto the beach. A crowd gathered, people milling about the turtle and backslapping the divers. Grunting with the effort, they hoisted the huge bulk over their heads and paraded up the beach towards an old pickup truck, the shouting crowd surrounding them.

Then it was quiet. I stood staring at the impression in the sand where the turtle had lain, struck dumb by all that had taken place. Looking out to sea I tried to conjure in my young imagination a turtle swimming under the ocean, and fish, and the rest of the creatures that lived in the ocean beyond my reach. I dreamed a boy's dream of capturing those creatures, of being an ocean hunter and of bringing the hidden gifts of the sea back for those on shore to see and eat.

The dream grew as I did. Soon I was able to live it, and the legacy of the Hawaiian divers appreciated beyond my wildest imaginings. Now, thirty five years later, the childhood vision has grown old, battered by cultural forces crueler than any sea. Yet it survives in me and its persistent flicker leads me to believe that it was not only right to follow that dream, it was necessary.

My watch is up and Ernie relieves me at the wheel. It is 1:20 AM and I go below to sleep, but can't. This trip has been a long time coming and sleep refuses to interfere. Returning topside, I offer to take the wheel. Ernie gives only token resistance, then stumbles back down to his bunk.

The moon is high on my port side. It appears

we are both headed in the same direction. Its light still dances, but on an ocean that has grown unexpectedly calm here in mid-channel. It is difficult to predict the moods of the ocean. We make our attempts, but in the end the ocean does what she wishes and we submit.

With all the knowledge that modern man carries with him, nature, especially the ocean, remains aloof and holds secrets which man instinctively feels he can never understand. Emerson observed, "Few adults can see nature." He knew that only the child's eye is wide and innocent enough to catch a glimpse of its fleeting magic. He also knew that the adult yearns for solid ground, for something to hang his hat on, confident that it will be there tomorrow. In the natural world there is only the immediate present: a fish breaks water and is gone, the gull descends on a school of bait, plucks one and retreats into the sun. Under the ocean such events occur in a dazzling array that only the schooled eye which has retained a sense of wonder can occasionally see.

The *Infinity* has found a steady ocean rhythm and her movement works my lubber legs, slowly kneading the unsteadiness away. Hour by hour my body sways in unison with the rocking boat and my land bound life drains away into the deck and is absorbed into the sea.

It is 4:30 AM and the sun appears to be forty-five minutes away from the horizon. A dim shape of the island looms before the bow. We are seven miles east of our destination, the isthmus, which lies high on the western portion of the island. Changing course, I run parallel with the shoreline, threading the ketch westward.

The sky is cloudless and the sun will be coming up bright and full on the island. It is already casting an orange glow against the cobalt blue sky in anticipation.

When I began coming regularly to the island eighteen years ago I was caught by the appeal of spending an entire summer here, living on a boat, hunting for my food and trading for the provisions that the sea could not provide. Now, with the reality before me, I feel unsure and have doubts. This was an idea born long ago when I was thoroughly absorbed in the ocean and blue water hunting. Much has changed. Perhaps this journey has come too late and is a mistake.

I watch the island grow and acquire dimension as the sun rises; the ambers and rusts take on a glow when the first light strikes its highest peaks. I've witnessed this same scene many times, waiting on a boat for enough sun so we could make out fish shapes in the early underwater light. The memory rekindles that excitement and my unanswerable doubts evaporate with the dawn.

Ernie wakes soon after the sun has ignited the hull on its starboard side. He arrives topside with coffee and we take in the early morning in silence. After our second cup he asks, "Do you have an anchorage in mind?"

"Not really. There are several possibilities. Let's see what turns up." Twenty minutes later we pass the cove called Rippers, which I had considered. It has a sandy bottom for anchoring and several good dive sites close by, but this Sunday it is filled with boats. Moving west up the island we peruse each likely looking cove, but for one reason or another reject them and continue on. We pass the isthmus, and every suitable cove we cross holds anchored boats. Then high cliffs come into view and resting beneath them, a deep cove. Despite two boats already at anchor, I know this will be the cove. We decide to wait the boats out, reasoning that they should leave in a few hours if they intend to reach the mainland before dark.

As the *Infinity* drifts three hundred yards off the cove, Ernie walks me through a short course on the care and maintenance of his beloved vessel: the electrical system, the plumbing, engine workings and a tour of the through hull fittings. By the end of our rounds we discover that the refrigeration system is down, there are problems with the electrical system, and the starter motor seems to have solenoid difficulties. It has been a while since this otherwise beautiful mahogany and teak boat has been to sea. I'm neither a mechanic nor an electrician, and there is more to this twenty-ton ketch than I understand. I begin to wonder what potential disasters lie beneath these newly discovered ailments. Will I be able to repair them if they choose to reveal themselves during the summer?

The two boats in the cove pull anchor five minutes apart, leaving it open to embrace the *Infinity*. We drop the bow anchor and swing into the cove, then row the skiff into shore and set the stern anchor twenty feet from the rocky beach. Returning to the *Infinity* we cinch up all lines, and within half an hour rest securely in what I came to learn was called Doctors Cove.

Fifty yards to the west of this beautiful cove a large kelp bed flows along the hundred-foot-high cliffs. Another smaller bed and reef lie twenty yards to the east and astern of the boat. Directly astern the rocky beach lifts to a twenty-foot incline where the land rolls into unscarred wheat colored hills that rise to twelve hundred feet at their highest points, and are dotted with scrub oak trees to their peaks.

Ernie and I spend our last hour sitting in the sun and enjoying the view. It is difficult to believe that it was just two months ago when I approached him with the idea of anchoring the *Infinity* at the island for four months where I would clean her up and fix whatever troubles her in exchange for the privilege of living on board in the primitive fashion I've chosen. Now on the threshold of the dream, the generosity of his gift hits with full force. Ernie's work keeps him from the sea these days, and I think that living vicariously through me will be as close to a voyage as he will be able to get for a while.

"Until you sever the bindings that keep you earth bound, and once again take to the ocean, I'll do my best to live this thing out for you and every other diver who ever wanted to make a similar journey."

Smiling, Ernie nods, "That's the idea."

When it is time for him to catch his ride back to the mainland, we hop into the yellow skiff and run east to the isthmus where the *Express* boat is waiting. We say our goodbyes on the dock and wish each other luck. Then Ernie jumps on the *Express*, which is at once underway, and I wait until it has passed Ship rock before returning to the skiff.

The fourteen-foot aluminum boat with its single occupant and new 25 horse outboard darts across the wind chopped sea, delivering me to the cove in fifteen minutes. Seeing the *Infinity* lying heavily at anchor conjures images of myself living on board for the summer. But they are nothing more than fuzzy speculations and I vow to keep my thoughts in the immediate present.

The ocean, wasting no time in its welcome, offers a taste of what is to come. White capped seas rise with a steady thirty knot wind, and the ketch rocks and rolls for three straight days and nights, making sleep impossible. On the second day the *Infinity*, taking her cue from the sea, begins to misbehave: the engine refuses to start and I need the voltage producing generator to recharge the batteries which power the lights, water pumps, radio and various other electricity drains. After several hours of frustrating investigation I locate the problem. The cable from the battery to the starter motor is severed at the connection, likely due to the jarring seas. The next day the plumbing begins to reveal leaks in both the head and galley. After a thorough cursing, I fix the leaks. In the afternoon the salon light falters and goes. The following morning I discover that the bilge pump has a short, and the starter solenoid continues to work only intermittently. The week is topped off when the stern line breaks loose in the heavy swells.

Busy from morning to evening, sleepless and on edge, I consider packing it in. But there is another side to these tribulations. My resourcefulness and sense of capability which have been lost over the last few years are being awakened and that discovery alone more than pays the fare.

By the sixth day the wind and the *Infinity* begin to settle down and for the first time since arriving, I sleep through the night. This rather inauspicious beginning has kept me out of the water. Having brought a minimum of supplies and with my protein goods already used up, I need to get into the ocean tomorrow and hunt for some food.

2

THE INSTRUMENT
OF THE HUNT

I suspect it was the Hawaiian waters that thinned my blood, because there is hardly a time during the year that I dive without a wet suit. Neither do the divers of Florida or Hawaii enjoy these waters after skinning it in their own tropics. They complain that the wet suit is bulky and that they lose a certain contact with the water that has become a part of the way they sense the ocean. I've become so familiar with the suit that it feels more like a second skin and I'm barely aware of it. But I know of what the warm water diver speaks and if given the choice, I too would go without the wet suit.

The sixty-three-degree waters of early June offer no choice, so with suit on, mask, fins, snorkel, gloves and weight belt all in place, and speargun in hand I ease over the side of the skiff and into the water. What a pleasure it is to feel the ocean again! This dense, moving environment is a living thing which pulls me down into itself, back into the womb of the great Mother Earth. The joy of being back in the water is accompanied by an uneasiness, like a meeting of old friends who have endured a long separation. There is an awkwardness in this initial reunion and I feel the stranger as I swim toward the kelp bed next to the cliffs.

Looking down from the surface to the sandy bottom of the cove, the view could easily be that of a barren desert seen from an altitude of ten thousand feet, broken occasionally by an oasis of green and scattered, half buried boulders. The visibility turns hazy as the water deepens and I drop down beneath the surface to where it opens up again and see the dark kelp bed off in the distance.

Kelp, in its many forms, is found along the western coast line of the continental United States. It continues to grow down the edge of the Baja peninsula until it meets with the warm water that inhibits its growth. It attaches to rocks, reefs and boulders with a strong root system that, in heavy surge, will often loosen the rock from its stronghold before the roots themselves break. Slender amber colored branches grow from the main stalk and produce broad textured leaves seven to ten inches wide. Attached to the branches, hollow pods the size of a thumb hold air which the plant extracts from the water, giving the kelp buoyancy and lifting its top branches to the surface. A mature plant can be well over ten feet wide and seventy feet high, and when the water is without current these kelp plants have the look of an amber forest of fragile trees.

The trees grow to the surface, then spread

across it, intertwining with the other kelp trees to create a heavy matted weaving, sometimes several feet thick, called a kelp bed.

These kelp forests provide the home, refuge and playground for a variety of Pacific coast fish: opaleye, catalina blues, blacksmiths, sheepshead, garibaldi, señoritas, anchovies and assorted perch. In this kingdom of the kelp forest the kelp bass, sometimes called the calico bass, reigns supreme. The calico averages three to four pounds in weight, although six- to eight-pounders are not uncommon. They grow as large as thirteen pounds and some divers have sworn to have seen them close to twenty pounds. The calico is marked with black and amber spots that give way to a white belly. The amber spots grow dark as the fish ages and a twelve-pound calico is almost solid black. Their markings give them a perfect camouflage for the kelp forest. A free swimming fish, the calico has an extraordinary sense of sight and hearing, and is defensively geared to react to sound (which travels five times faster in the water than in air) and to movement. Its sensory systems miss nothing. Every little bump and bubble is recorded and every movement, however slight, is perceived. These are not the senses of the dimwitted; calicos are extremely intelligent and they augment their resources with the reaction time of a hummingbird. The calico's firm white meat is the best tasting in the kelp forest.

Within every active kelp forest lies a defensive network that is loosely formed by the collective eyes and ears of the free swimming fish that reside there. When a fish senses either by sight, sound or vibration a potential threat, it bolts away, alerting other fish in the vicinity that all is not safe in the forest. The hunter, be it seal or man, must pass through this warning system without detection if it or he is to secure a meal.

Moving unnoticed within this ultrasensitive world is difficult. Unlike man, the seal need not concern itself with air trapped inside a wet suit, fins, or booties that releases underwater tell-tale bubbles. The seal, designed for the water, is fast and fluid and does not make the subtle noises that man must work to avoid. Both man and seal are equally visible in their movement though, and in the stillness of a kelp forest it is movement which attracts the eye of the calico. The seal uses its speed and maneuverability to acquire its food. Without those capabilities man must use his knowledge of the fishes' habits and have a well developed stalking technique in order to be an effective hunter in the forest.

The patterns of my swimming and breathing change when I near the edge of the kelp bed, fins kept as much beneath the surface as possible, breaths taken in quiet shallow rhythm. Using the light current I drift onto the edges of the kelp and then into the bed itself, gliding around the maze of floating kelp that rests thickly on the surface. Looking down, I see fish at various depth levels, all intent with their business and play. Some notice me; others are unaware of my presence. Continuing to drift in toward the heart of the bed, I come to a point where I can no longer progress on the surface due to the spreading kelp. Hyperventilating for twenty seconds, then turning as if to go into a handstand, I descend face first into the forest, hanging momentarily just beneath the surface to allow the excess air in my suit to clear. Then I glide off through the kelp trees like a giant wingless bird descending into a grove of amber redwoods. Leveling off at neutral buoyancy, a depth of twenty-two feet, and suspended in the stillness, I look into the azure blue, where the golden trees ascend from the ocean floor to a crystal ceiling. Within the deepening forest lie clearings bare of the growing kelp, and with the light from above, these large rooms, some twenty feet in diameter, walled with thick kelp from bottom to top, glow blue-green. Often these "rooms" house calico bass and other fish of the kelp forest which like to congregate in the warmth of the afternoon sun. The fish feel secure in these open spaces because they cannot be easily taken by the seals which, like man, use the kelp for cover, and strike quickly from a short distance.

As I move toward the nearest room the dense kelp conceals my approach. Peering around a large stalk five feet from its perimeter, I see several calicos along with opaleye, señoritas, Catalina blues and a school of anchovy hanging in the warmth of their sanctuary. All of the larger fish are facing in my direction as though I had knocked on a door. The fish, knowing they are out of speargun range (calicos have an uncanny facility for knowing the precise range for a variety of spearguns), wait for me to make a move. I do, and they evaporate quickly behind a wall of kelp. Out of air, I kick my way to the surface. On top, recapturing my breath, I drift over to the next dense area of kelp. After several minutes I descend again, pulling my snorkel out of my mouth with the last breath so no noise is made by the escaping bubbles. Gliding down along a large kelp tree which covers my descent, I'm met by a school of a dozen opaleye. The school freezes for an instant in eye contact, then turns as a single unit moving quickly in the opposite direction. To my right is another room and I slide toward it, weaving through the lush forest. Six feet from its perimeter I carefully peek into the open space. There are a dozen fish in the interior, all warming themselves in the sun-sprayed room. Among them are two large calicos, and again all are staring in my direction. I remain motionless on the fringe. The smaller fish become curious and move unafraid toward me. The big calicos know my intentions and wander off into the kelp. Hanging on the periphery of the kelp room, I feel out of touch with the ocean and thoroughly inept in my stalking. Unmoving, I remain on the edge of the kelp room until my need for air forces me to the surface. Floating on top I realize how far away from this world I've been and wonder how long it will be before I can reconnect with it again.

When it is done right, underwater stalking is like a dance. There is a rhythm. Moving up and down, anticipating the movements of the fish, constantly reading the environment, breathing and not breathing. There are miles to go before I dance that dance again. Fortunately I have the best stalking instructors in the ocean at my disposal: the calicos themselves. Their teaching methods are clear and direct. The slightest noise will alert them to my presence. If I am clumsy and thrash about on the surface or on my descent, the disturbance is likely to drive them off before visual contact is ever made. When the visibility does permit visual contact then both sound and movement become critical. If the fish catches sight of the hunter first, it is generally conceded to be too late to stalk the fish. Occasionally the hunter, through luck and a bit of trickery, can get near enough for a shot after the fish has seen him. But it is extremely difficult, for at that point direct eye contact will certainly spook the fish. He must observe it exclusively through his peripheral vision. Moving with imperceptible slowness, he can mesmerize the fish into forgetting the threat by becoming a floating statue. Still this is not enough; elements of luck must also fall into place: the breath hold at the moment of the sighting, the depth of the fish, the position of the fish, and the angle of the speargun at the time of the sighting (for it cannot be moved to any degree without alerting the fish). All of these must come together and accompany an errorless stalk and a well placed arrow.

At the moment my noise is alerting the fish, and my ability to move unseen is ineffectual. My eyes are slow to spot a fish and the calicos are seeing me before I see them. Several have already squirted away, sounding for the safety of deep water.

A hunter can have all the technique and knowledge that is available to a human being, but if he has not learned to see, he will never be a spearfisherman. One cannot smell or rarely hear a fish, certainly never touch one and the tasting is done long after the outcome of the event has been determined. Seeing the fish before it sees you: that is the first precept of spear-fishing. I've met many an enthusiastic diver who passionately

wanted to be a hunter of fish. I'd show him everything I knew, but in the end he could never spot a
fish until it was too late. His eye was unable to
penetrate the busy, entangled world that lies beneath the surface and separate the fish from its
concealed place: a part of a tail fin in a cave, the
top edge of a dorsal fin rising above a seaweed
encrusted rock, a shadow that does not fit into
the seascape, the quarter inch of exposed tail slot-
ted between a gathering of kelp leaves. When hunting the shallows of a coast line, it is the eyes of
the spearfisherman that ultimately determine the
success or failure of his efforts.

Both the fish and the environment dictate the
hunter's every move. Stalking a fish is a matter of
being able to respond instantly and correctly to
the fish's movement or position within the environment. The proper response is learned by years
of observing the fish's habits and characteristics
within the ever changing environment. These observations and the hunter's movement in response
to those observations guide him to his opportunities.

Still moving west, I'm now three hundred yards
from the *Infinity*. My absence from the ocean is
glaringly reflected in a parade of stalking mistakes. Moving to within range (ten feet) of a good
sized calico, a slight movement of my gloved hand
catches the fish's eye and it, along with every fish
in the area, explodes away as though they are si-
multaneously shocked by the same electrical current. There is no margin for error when stalking
fish. The slightest mistake is as costly as the clum-
siest blunder. When a section of the forest is
startled into flight like this, all fish are put on

guard and there is no point in remaining in the area.

All the care taken in the stalk comes to nothing if the shot is not true. In spearfishing the shot is perhaps more critical than in any other form of hunting. If a land animal is wounded and then runs off into a forest or thicket, its blood spoor can be followed and the animal can eventually be tracked down. A wounded fish simply swims away and the spearfisherman, unable to track it, looses it to the haze or a well hidden cave. For this reason only a good, clear shot should be attempted, with particular emphasis on accuracy—which, in this split second environment, is considerably easier said than done.

Wounded fish, if not struck in the gut or the head or the backbone, have an amazing facility for recuperation. I once speared a large calico, close to ten pounds. The shot was high and hit just above the backbone, which would normally be considered good placement, but the fish fought wildly against the spear shaft and before I could get a hand in its gills, it escaped, tearing an enormous chunk of flesh from the top of the backbone to its dorsal fin. No land animal could have survived such a wound. Six months later, hunting the same bed, I saw the fish again. It was somewhat slimmer, but its terrible wound had completely healed.

The ideal placement for an arrow is just behind the midpoint of the gill plate. It is a solid area where the backbone meets with the head. If the shot is too low, the arrow will pierce the belly and the fish will tear off and surely die. Too high and the fish, unhurt, will wrestle free if the hunter cannot quickly get a hand on it. The same holds true for a shot placed near the tail. Head shots are tricky because the area is small, and accuracy must be pin-point. Aiming a speargun calls for great concentration, for he who sees the whole fish will almost certainly miss the shot. I try to focus on a spot just behind the gill plate that is no larger than a dime. That is all I see. There is so little time to aim, that as soon as that spot is lined up and I am within range, the trigger is pulled.

The hunting tool I am using for these smaller fish is hand made and resembles something between a cross bow and a 17th century musket. It operates much like the cross bow, but instead of a single cord stretching back and releasing the arrow, two nearly solid bands of 9/16" diameter rubber tubing are pulled to eighty pounds of pressure to propel the arrow when the trigger is released. The square stock or barrel on which the arrow rests is made of mahogany. It is four feet long and 1-3/4" on a side. This speargun's effective range is seven to ten feet. Like the musket, it holds one shot. The spent arrow must be retrieved and refit into the trigger housing, the shooting line restrung, and the rubber slings pulled back to their notches on the arrow. The procedure takes a minute or two, and by the time the gun is set up again the fish in the area have long fled. There are no second chances, and I've come to prefer it that way. It calls for nothing less than total concentration and a keen mental edge is the result. All ocean predators live and die on this edge. I see no reason why it should be any different for me.

Several years ago the Department of Fish and

Game in California undertook a study to determine the efficiency of ocean spearfishing. They
found it to be the least effective method of all those
available for acquiring fish. Jacques Cousteau
states that man could not survive through
spearfishing, that the hunter would spend more
energy in the attempt than he could replace by
the food he speared. If I continue to hunt as I have,
I'll soon become another statistic in support of
Cousteau's observation. Fortunately there are
enough fish in these kelp beds to allow for my
mistakes. Eventually I spear a small calico, filling my immediate needs.

The *Infinity* is out of sight, lost behind a bend
in the cliffs. I've been in the water for almost three
hours and the cold is beginning to creep into my
bones. To make better time on my return, I swim
out of the maze of kelp and into the open water
on the outside. The water is deep and the bottom
has disappeared into an opaque blue. Dropping
down for a look, I see a sand bottom at sixty feet
with the edge of the kelp growing right to it. Halfway down I get the full view and know I've entered another country. There is a tension in this
open water that contrasts sharply with the unhurried pace in the kelp forest. Here is where the
pelagics run, the yellowtail, white sea bass, barracuda, bonito, shark and whale. Here begins the
vast wilderness of blue water.

Moving down the outside edge of the kelp, I see
large calicos lying motionless, eyeing the bait from
the deep fringe. They are on the hunt. The sun
has settled behind the cliffs and the predators are
beginning to stir. The calicos see me as I descend
and retreat into the forest. The schools of baitfish,

huddled tightly into small balls, are moving nervously just beneath the surface. They are the bread and butter of the pelagics; their time is almost upon them. The cold keeps me swimming and I'm unable to wait for the drama of the evening feed to unfold. The excitement of the blue water is undeniable. It charges me up and lifts me to another level of alertness, and for a time it warms my cold bones.

***

The next four days I return to the kelp beds and to my teachers, the calicos. Each day is different: the visibility fluctuates, the current changes tempo as well as direction, the sun pops in and out of the clouds and the tides are in a continual state of flux. Each factor or combination of factors in some way affects the inhabitants of the kelp forest, and I adjust to these changes accordingly. If a current is running, the calicos tend to take refuge beneath the bent kelp trees and face into the current, so I too must face into the current, swimming beneath the bent kelp looking up left and right for the hidden fish. If the visibility closes down, then I'll dive deeper, moving slowly, looking up toward the sun for silhouettes of the fish, rather than trying to see them from the surface when the water is clear. There are variables within variables and sometimes the changes become so subtle that I'm not sure why I respond to the environment as I do, or why I follow a particular course to a fish, or how I determine there was a fish there at all.

Each day shows improvement. Old instincts

reawake and forgotten knowledge resurfaces. By the end of my first week in the water my awkwardness has disappeared, my bottom time has increased and I feel more like an insider looking out than an outsider looking in. Still, there are miles to go before my response to the fish and the environment becomes second nature.

As the rough edges smooth out both in the water and on board, I take the opportunity to give the yellow hulled skiff a new name. The boat's old name, *Yellow Snow*, was the choice of its previous owner, and with new beginnings before us, the time has come to erase its past. Without new letters to replace the old ones I've decided to remove the Y, E, L, and S, leaving the name *Low Now*. While scraping off the old letters, I think of the boatmen who spend quiet afternoons on the after deck of their craft looking for hidden messages within the names of other pleasure boats. The *Low Now* has no message. The words make no sense, an unanswerable riddle for the yachting folk to ponder in their summer afternoons.

Actually that isn't quite right; there is a meaning to the nonsense, a message perhaps a cryptographer could decipher. But to do it, he would have to know something about me. He would have to know that for most of my adult life I've been trying to fit into a society that has made little sense to me. And I have undoubtedly made even less sense to it. You see, I was born a hunter. Some folks are born musicians, or artists, or athletes. Others are born to make money, heal people, design buildings and bridges, tend bar, and sail ships. There are those born to no particular calling at all, and slide through life untroubled by such pullings. Although I find it hard to believe that there are men (and women) born to be accountants, sell insurance, be ushers, or in general wear wing tip shoes, they at least are able to make their way in life. When they are out of a job, they can, with a degree of assurance, run down to the unemployment office and ask, "Have you got anything for me today?" There is no employment available for blue water hunters; take my word for it.

I've tried all sorts of jobs, white collar, blue collar, no collar. I've even worn wing tip shoes. Every serious job I had ate me alive. The more money I made, the bigger chunks it took out of me. Not chunks of flesh; I could have lived with that. What is taken cannot be seen with the naked eye. What is taken is pieces of the spirit, slices of the soul, cuts of the heart. What is taken is who you are.

In all my time spent in the ocean wilderness, it has never once asked for nor taken a piece of me. Quite the reverse: it has healed that which was wounded; it has given freely of its gifts and asks only that I pay close attention to it. Upon my entry into the ocean, it fills my spirit, cleanses my soul and repairs my tattered heart. And therein lies the cryptic message of the *Low Now*, and the reason I am here.

***

Tuesday morning, after working the kelp bed for fish, I swim along the rocky shoreline inside the bed next to the cliffs, optimistically prowling the holes and crevices for abalone that might have been overlooked by the hordes of divers who come to Catalina every year searching for this rich delicacy. The abalone attaches itself to the rocky surfaces with a powerful muscle called a foot. This muscle, when cut into quarter-inch slices, pounded tender with a serrated mallet, then breaded and briefly cooked, is delicious. Abalone are scarce these days, and finding the few that have escaped the abalone bar is becoming more difficult each year.

There was a time, not a dozen years ago, when the abalone were still plentiful and considered an afterthought to a day of diving. Returning from a morning of spearfishing, we would pick up our limit of five each in ten minutes. In the late 40's and early 50's the abalone were as thick as barnacles on a mooring cable. Wally Potts of San Diego once brought up a limit in one dive. Finding them stacked five deep, all Wally had to do was pry off the bottom ab and he had his limit. Today the limit is four and if a diver doesn't have a bed scouted out for himself, he may spend hours, even days, looking for abalone and still come up empty.

It has been suggested that the tremendous number of SCUBA divers over the last twenty years have accounted for the demise of the abalone. To a degree that is correct, but the SCUBA divers are not entirely to blame. The commercial abalone divers finished off these waters during the 70's. As the price of abalone increased, so did their efforts. By the end of the 70's there weren't enough abalone left to make a profit. The California Department of Fish and Game has placed a moratorium on selected areas and are restocking old habitats with farm-bred juveniles. Despite their efforts, we shall never again see these shellfish as abundant as they once were.

Diving down into the fifteen-foot shallows of the rocky shoreline and brushing back the dense seaweed and bottom kelp that grows in crowded gardens I poke around the holes and tunnels that honeycomb the boulder-strewn bottom. After forty minutes I've seen scores of eels but not a single legal sized abalone.

Like most ardent free divers I've probably taken more foolish chances pulling out abalone than just about anything I've done in the ocean, wiggling into the back of some small cave or narrow opening that tunnels down into a hole buried deep inside a crush of boulders, then stretching one arm to its full extension to slip the flat fourteen-inch iron bar between the abalone and its rock and lifting, with considerable force, to break its powerful grip, then blindly reaching for it before trying to back out of the tight space I have squeezed myself into.

Now every other hole has an eel in it, and the abalone are gone. The eels have become one of those rare oddities in the natural world: a species that has not diminished over the years but, by all appearances, has increased. What message is nature giving us when the scavengers now dominate where others once prospered?

Eventually I discover a small cache of black abalone which, because of their toughness and small size, are left alone by both sport and commercial divers. There is no sign of the coveted pinks and greens. I also come across an adolescent eel which has wedged itself head first into a small hole and left six inches of tail exposed. The temptation is irresistible: I reach out and give the tail a pinch. It instantly flies into a frenzied panic

that reveals its owner's predicament; the eel is
either stuck or is unwilling to back out of the hole
and turn around. The tail wiggles and squirms
wildly in an attempt to elude its unseen attacker.
I leave it gyrating crazily, unable to make up its
mind. The creatures of the ocean are always in
such control of themselves seeing this eel trying
to escape from the jaws of its own imagination
strikes me as hilarious. After spending a week in
the kelp forests the instrument of the hunt may
not have been retooled, but I've removed much of
the rust. My thoughts float in blue water and I'm
anxious to return to it. Stalking the kelp forest is
as different from stalking blue water as hunting
rabbits is from hunting bear.

Every kelp bed usually holds a few calicos. If
one bed is barren or has been spooked, there is
always another twenty yards up the line. Stalking pelagic game fish is another matter entirely.
These fish are continually on the move and only
come into certain areas for brief moments to feed.
The trick is to know where these areas are and at
what time the fish might breeze by for a meal.

Starlight, Eagle Reef, Ship Rock, Two Goats,
Isthmus Reef, and the east and west ends of the
island have been the sites where the white sea
bass and yellowtail have been seen over the years.
At one time or another all of these areas have
produced fish. Now everything has changed. The
fish have thinned out, and much of the bait is gone.
It will be difficult to find fish even if I knew where
to look. Two Goats, an old favorite, pops into my
head and I decide to give it a try. If nothing turns
up, I'll jump over to Eagle and work my way east.

The speargun used for these game fish is simi-

lar in style to the one used for calico. It is a foot
longer and holds an additional band of 9/16" rubber tubing for a total of three bands, each band
producing a hundred pounds of pressure when
pulled back into cocking position. Its effective
range is fifteen feet, although shots of twenty feet
have brought fish to my hand. I try to avoid taking long shots because the risk of losing a fish
becomes greater in proportion to the distance the
arrow travels. In and around the kelp I use a reel
holding a hundred and fifty feet of five hundred-
pound test nylon line. The reel is attached to the
stock in a similar position as on a fishing rod. Aside
from the trigger mechanism, which is manufac-
tured in Australia, this speargun is entirely handmade.

The hardware includes a stainless steel heat
treated arrow with a detachable tip which is connected by eighteen inches of stainless cable to a
slide ring which encircles the arrow. All hardware
on this speargun is fabricated by one of the original fathers of diving, Charlie Sturgill.

Many blue water hunters design and build their
own spearguns to fit their particular physical
characteristics and hunting needs. A good number of hours is given to the crafting of a speargun,
yet attachment to it must be minimal. Several
years ago in Mexico, two brothers, Jerry and Dan
Higman, were hunting grouper in the gulf. Jerry
heard the arrow release from his brother's
speargun and seconds later a large grouper came
charging down a sharp dropoff heading into deep
water. Twenty feet behind and holding on to his
newly built teak and mahogany gun came Dan,
being pulled to the depths. His shooting line was

half hitched around the muzzle and the pressure was too great for him to pull in slack and release the line. Shortly the priorities righted themselves and Dan surrendered his speargun and returned to the surface. He couldn't tell me if it was easier to let go of a new speargun rather than an old one; he simply said that you had better be willing to let it go.

Each spearfisherman, like most fishermen and hunters, has an opinion about what period of the day is best to seek out game. Some prefer the morning when the chilly water turns the fish lethargic and they are somewhat easier to approach. I'm partial to the late afternoon when the hunger tension begins to build, reaching its peak just before dark. You can almost feel the fish before you see them. The bait fish are fidgety; the free swimmers pick up their pace and there is electricity in the water. It is a time when the ocean is wildly alive, when the dimming light continually alters perspective and breeds expectations packaged in that ghostly blue that can produce anything.

The sun has been eclipsed by gray clouds and it seems later than it is. I dress into my wet suit, then load the gear into the *Low Now*. The outboard fires up on one pull and I head east to Two Goats. The *Low Now* surfs across the wind chopped sea at three-quarter throttle, easily outracing the swift following sea. In ten minutes I cut the engine and let the skiff glide silently into Two Goats, then gently lower the anchor so as not to disturb any fish that might be lolling nearby.

The water is diveable, clear enough to see the sandy bottom of the cove at thirty-five feet. Following the kelp line from the anchored boat, I swim out to a far point of kelp that lies in fifty-five feet of water. There is slight current running east to west. The pelagics generally like to swim into the current so should be moving west to east. After hyperventilating I drop down, hesitating for a moment to clear my suit of air then descend to twenty-two feet, and hang in the stillness to read the area. The kelp bed lies behind me. There are two very tall, sparse kelp trees forty feet away on the deep outside. A large concentration of baitfish, packed into separate schools, drifts between me and the outside stalks. Several large calicos give me an obligatory look from the fringe of the bed, then swim back into the shelter of the forest. Smaller calicos draw close and observe the early evening activities. Schools of opaleye and croaker move nervously in and out of the fringe. Two medium sized calico swim across the stretch of blue water from the outside strands of kelp for a quick investigation, then retreat. I return to the surface, having been thoroughly scrutinized.

The fish that remain in the area sense that they are in no danger and accept my presence. Swimming over to the bait fish and diving down, I look for nicks or chew marks on their thin silver-blue bodies, which indicate that predators have been working the school. I find none, nor are the fish skittish when I close to within several feet of them.

Back on top I watch the bait while recapturing my breath. The second school farther out and to my left dashes toward the bed, alerting all that something is about. I drop down facing the disturbance and watch two sturdy yellowtail cruise into the empty space where the bait have just

been. Continuing to drop, I level off at the same
depth as the yellows and turn, facing ninety degrees away from them with the speargun pointed
out into empty water. The characteristic curiosity of the fish should be aroused and bring them
swimming parallel to my left side. Then if they
follow the script, they will make a pass directly
in front of me and in that brief moment, should
come within range. The fish respond to form and
move toward me, then make their turn. It is wider
than I had anticipated, leaving me out of position.
Swimming ahead six feet, I regain position, quar-
tering the lead fish off in the process, and let the
arrow fly. The fish is moving quickly and the arrow strikes several inches past mid-body; in full
acceleration the yellowtail powers out to sea.
Grabbing the line which is spinning off the reel, I
am yanked down several feet by the force of the
speeding fish. Kicking hard toward the surface, I
release line grudgingly until reaching the top.
Here my additional buoyancy gives me an advantage, and I work the yellow, pulling the line in to
me, as one might pull on the lead of a stubborn
pony. Several minutes later, with a hand finally
on the arrow I guide the fish to me, slipping my
other hand into its gills.

In the water just fifteen minutes and the
ocean generously provides a fine yellowtail. Back
in the *Low Now* I'm surprised and pleased with
my response during the stalk. Old instincts took
over, and it did not seem as though I had a thought
throughout the entire episode; if I had I probably
would have missed the fish altogether.

I've long ceased taking full credit for the fish
the ocean provides. The ocean is too vast, rich and

powerful an entity for me to assume that in any way I have conquered it. At best the effort is co-operative, with nature supplying the sustenance and I the means to capture it. When the land was as bountiful as the ocean the hunting peoples understood the enormous and benevolent power of nature and became connected to that power through the animals they hunted. That understanding has disappeared with the wildlife. Out here on a frothing ocean in a pounding boat, with the glowing colors of a setting sun in my face and a noble fish at my feet, the power of nature and my connection to it in the form of nourishment are wonderfully evident.

3

THE FATHERS

The Hawaiians, with their play in the surf and their boldness past the surf line, made my transition from land creature to sea creature easy. Imitating the older boys, I silently battled the dragons of the mind and dove down into the mysterious water to pluck some small treasure from the shallows. Soon the dragons disappeared and the mysterious became a moving wonderland that pulled at my curiosity.

Had my life been launched inland and away from any ocean influences, and had I come upon the great Pacific for the first time as an adult, I would have found a considerable barrier lying just past the surf line. Swimming to it, I would have tread water on leaden legs, unable to move farther with any degree of comfort.

This first barrier is a preliminary response to the gut feeling that one is trespassing into unknown and dangerous territory. Somewhere between the sandy bottom of the shore and the deep water where no bottom can be seen at all lies the true obstruction, one forged of materials that have existed throughout human history. It is built on a foundation of myth and misconception. The great bulk of it rests in the fear of the unknown and its power lies in man's awareness of his vulnerability within the environment. These elements generate a force that keeps the land dweller within reach of his steadfast shore. Like Cerebus, the monstrous three-headed dog, mythical guardian of the underworld, the shark is the sentinel of the deep ocean. It, more than any other ocean inhabitant, has kept man from enthusiastically probing the undersea world. The shark embodies the darkest terror within man: his vulnerability. He cannot run from the shark, or climb a tree, or throw a stone or cast a spear in his defense. And if he could, where would he strike? The shark has no bones to break, no exposed arteries to sever and will swim for days after its belly has been ripped open. There is no other creature on the planet to which man is more physically and psychologically vulnerable. To advance into the deep ocean the first men had to encounter the shark on both these fronts.

Pioneers are heralded, if for nothing else, for their courage. They go beyond the established limits and push into the dark unknown. From Eric the Red to Colombus, from Marco Polo to Daniel Boone, and from Charles Lindberg to John Glenn, the list reads as a history of mankind's accomplishments. Buried and almost invisible on that list are the first men to break through the deep ocean barriers and probe the blue water wilderness. These men were the forerunners to the SCUBA revolution. They were the first to defy the ancient myths and topple the stone pillars of fear. They led land bound man into this planet's oceans and seas.

By all accounts, it was just over fifty years ago, in the late 20's and early 30's, that western man began to make his way out beyond the water's edge. Like the ancient others who first penetrated unfamiliar territory, these men were hunters.

Those closest to the ocean in the late 20's were the men and boys of the beach who swam in the water, bodysurfed the shorebreak waves and took their paddleboards out past the surf line. They were called beach boys in Hawaii and watermen on the California and Florida coasts. In California these watermen knew which rocky beach yielded the rich abalone that had pushed its way into knee deep water. Low tide was the time to pluck these delicacies from their hiding places beneath the rocks and between the cracks and crevices. Throughout the 20's the watermen worked the shoreline for abalone until, in more heavily populated areas, the free meals ran out.

In 1931 Charlie Sturgill began to wade out past the shoreline where, in waist deep water, he continued to pursue the abundant abalone. Blindly feeling his way along, Charlie was often spiked by unseen lobster and occasionally bitten by eels, but he was a tough bird and a few nips on the fingers didn't slow him down.

"I had a pretty good system worked out. I used a wooden barrel stuck down into an inner tube of a truck tire and when I filled the barrel up with abs it was usually too heavy for me to push back to the beach. So my wife Laura would pull it in with a line from the shore."

While Charlie was pulling abalone out by the barrel full in Los Angeles county, ninety miles south, down in San Diego, a small colony of watermen was doing much the same thing. Jack Prodanovitch, Glenn Orr and Ben Stone were frustrated by their inability to see underwater. They knew there were more abalone down there, more than their most extravagant visions could conceive.

In 1933 the three located some swimmers' goggles, the kind long distance swimmers use to keep the water out of their eyes. Although the goggles were not designed for seeing underwater, the men tried using them for that purpose. The goggles kept the water out, but they also created double vision because the glass was not in a straight plane across the eye holes. Jack could see when he kept one eye closed, but he had no depth of field and eventually the disadvantages of this distorted view prodded him into the construction of his own diving goggles, which he made out of radiator hose. The problem of lens alignment still plagued him and this failure gave light to the idea that perhaps a large single piece of glass could be used like a mask.

"I found an oblong shaped piece that came from the instrument panel of an old Pierce Arrow. It had the amp meter etched on the top and the oil gauge etched on the bottom, and I used a copper shell to house the glass on one end and fixed a rubber cushion on the other end to seal it to my face. It leaked badly but it worked better than the goggles."

Soon Jack, Glen and Ben began bringing in sack-
fuls of the now visible abalone. In the process they
discovered that the lobster of the Pacific coast
were almost as abundant as the abalone.

As the San Diego trio were getting their first
blurry look at the Pacific, Earl Pinder, Chief of
Life Guards in Miami Beach Florida, was initiat-
ing his three sons, Don, Fred, and little Art, into
the undersea life of the Florida waters. There are
no abalone in the tropics. The boys' motivation to
dive came from a different source. They could look
down into the warm, crystal clear water off of the
Miami jettys and see fish of many colors and species cruising along in the shallow water. The
Pinders' equipment was as crude as the Pacific
Coast divers': they constructed their masks out
of cut glass and used the soft rubber of inner tubes
(real rubber in those days) to seal the masks to
their faces. These masks, like those of their unknown brothers in the west, leaked badly and had
to be cleared of water after every dive, but it was
a beginning. In fact, it was the beginning for
spearfishing on this continent.

The Pinders had what no one else in the United
States possessed, an effective hunting tool—the
primitive Hawaiian sling. The simplest of instru-
ments, the sling was no more than a hollow bam-
boo tube six inches long with a length of inner
tube attached to one end, forming a sling. The free
shaft or arrow (made from the stays of old um-
brellas) slipped through the tube and into the
rubber sling then was pulled back and released
in one motion, identical to the bow and arrow. The
simplicity of the Hawaiian sling belies the difficulty in its mastery, and the boys spent much of

their time retrieving misspent arrows from the rocks of the Miami jettys.

In the summer of '34 Charlie got wind of a Santa Monica lifeguard, Bill O'Conner, who was making diving goggles out of fire hose and round glass lenses. He bought a pair and had the same lens distortions that Jack experienced down in San Diego. They hurt and leaked, yet despite the drawbacks Charlie doubled his abalone take and began pinching a few lobsters on the side.

Then in 1935 a major breakthrough occurred on the Pacific Coast. An acquaintance of Jack's, a truck driver, was picking up a load of hardware in an old warehouse on Terminal Island in San Pedro. Among the crates and boxes he spotted a Japanese face mask. He brought it back to San Diego for Jack's inspection and sea trial. The mask sealed tightly around his face and he was able to make repeated dives without it filling with sea water. During that same year, independent of Jack's discovery, Charlie also came across a Japanese face mask and for really the first time the Pacific Coast clearly revealed itself to the eyes of a breath hold diver.

The Pinders sharpened their skills with the difficult sling from Miami Beach to Soldiers Key. The clear water begged for underwater hunting. They could spear a fish, watch it swim away to a hole or crevice, follow the fish from the surface, then dive down and retrieve it. In Florida and other clear water areas, (the Caribbean and South Pacific) the Hawaiian sling could be used effectively. In the cloudy waters of the Pacific and Atlantic the sling was not a practical hunting tool. A fish speared with a free arrow could easily swim out of view, or the arrow, having missed its mark, would disappear and be lost in the gloom. In 1936, while the California divers worked the abalone and lobster, seven-year-old Art Pinder speared a seven and a half-pound snook, his first big fish with the sling.

With masks on their faces, gloves on their hands and sneakers on their feet, the boys of the Pacific began to harvest the coastline shallows. I asked Charlie what the limit was for abalone and lobster.

"Hell, there wasn't no game wardens in them days—your limit was as much as you could carry back to your car. Back then I would take only four or five lobsters—'course they weighed fifteen to twenty pounds apiece. First time I saw one of those real big ones they looked like they could get you instead of you getting them. But it didn't take us long to figure out how to get a hold of them so they wouldn't pull your face mask off or womp you good where it hurts. Most of what we got was in five or six feet of water, and the bigger ones always seemed to be just a little deeper than we could reach."

The abundant lobster and abalone slowly pulled the Pacific divers into deeper water. The virgin coastline lay before them, teeming with new and unfamiliar forms of life, and their unschooled eyes caught bits and pieces of the fecundity that millions of unmolested years could bring. At first they saw only the obvious: abalone covering every rock and hard place, and where there was no space the abalone climbed on the backs of those already secured. They saw the nocturnal lobsters crawling around the bottom in broad daylight, and thousands more crammed into every available crack and crevice that wasn't taken up by abalone or scallops. There were no vacancies in 1936.

After a time the divers' eyes adjusted to the underwater busyness, and for the next few years they studied the ocean inhabitants, learned their ways, and in the process grew comfortable themselves in these new surroundings.

Soon the abing and lobstering began to wear thin. They could easily pull out all they wanted and the challenge was diminishing. In their explorations the divers were beginning to see a variety of fish: sand bass, croaker, corbina, perch and halibut, plus a myriad of others whose names they had not yet learned. Whatever it is that separates the food gatherer from the hunter called to them.

In the summer of 1937 the Pacific divers of San Diego and Los Angeles independently began to experiment with pole spears. Charlie used a five-foot broom handle with a five-fined frog gig attached to one end. Jack and his new diving partner, Wally Potts, had ten-foot poles using the same gig. Like the spears of the early hunters of the land theirs were powered by arm strength alone. Despite the difficulty they began to bring in small croaker, sand bass, corbina, perch and halibut. By the end of the summer of 1938 underwater spearfishing had established itself on the Pacific coast.

The pole spear sparked a new enthusiasm and through the next year the divers, diving as often as possible, learned the language of the fish and began to see the interrelationships between the free swimmers and the environment. After a while they started to connect the pieces of this giant puzzle. As hunters do, they formed a picture of how the underwater environment operates. The more complete the picture, the better the hunter. Eventually the ocean lived in their senses and memories. More importantly, it lived in their intuition.

As this intuition grew, it became the source that led the hunter down the untrodden paths of a new territory with some understanding of what might lie unseen before him. In the summer of 1939, Jack and Wally found themselves on such a path. One of those rare and unexplained quirks of nature provided the motivation for these men to make a quantum leap from the relative shallows of Boomer Beach to the blue waters of the Pacific.

Boomer Beach lies in the picturesque coastal town of La Jolla, California, ten miles north of San Diego. For years surf fishermen, after a particularly long cast, would hook into something so strong it would strip the line off a reel and the fisherman would be powerless to stop it. This had happened enough times that a bit of a legend formed within the cluster of fishermen who regularly wet their lines there in the surf. Jack and Wally had heard the stories and one day after an abalone dive, encouraged by their dive buddy, Glenn Orr, they decided to investigate. They swam straight out to where the sand began to drop off into a kelpy boulder-ridden bottom and almost immediately saw the fish that proved to have the greatest influence on the San Diego divers. The fish was estimated to weigh close to two hundred pounds. Both Jack and Wally mis-identified it as a Jew fish. Only later after describing it to marine biologist Dr. Carl Hubbs of Scripps Institute of Oceanography did they learn it was a broomtail grouper, which was news in itself because grouper are not found in the cold waters of the Pacific. As it turned out there were enough grouper at Boomer Beach to form a sizeable colony. Since that discovery in 1939 no other grouper have been found on the coast of California. Perhaps, as some suggest, the grouper ranged up and down the Pacific for thousands of years, and this was their last remaining settlement. There is no way to know how long they had been residing there or why or how they came to settle in that single cove.

Jack and Wally never imagined that a fish could grow to such a size and be so close to shore. The sighting generated unbridled excitement and they set out to land the broomtail.

They knew nothing of the strength and power of a big fish, and didn't have a clue as to how to handle it. Jack describes his and Wally's first attempt to spear the grouper. "We located a fish—I'm sure it wasn't the same one—in about thirty feet of water and I got on one side of the fish, which looked to weigh a hundred and fifty pounds, and Wally got on the other side. Our plan was to swim down on either side of the grouper and shove our five pronged spears into it as hard as we could. Well, we dove down and I took my spear and pushed down into the fish with everything I had, and Wally did the same. It was like hitting a bag of wet cement. The fish swam off as if nothing happened."

This failure drew Jack and Wally into their second love: the research and development of big game spearfishing equipment.

"We sat around for days trying to figure out how

in the world we could build something that would
stop a big fish like that and work effectively underwater. There were so many factors that had to
be explored. The five pronged spear was useless.
What we needed was a head that would penetrate
the fish's body, and in these murky waters we also
had to have some kind of retrieval system."

While Jack and Wally explored the possibilities
for spearing a fish that in power alone dwarfed
them collectively in the water, a 1932 Olympic gold
medal winner in sailing, Owen Churchill, was enjoying an excursion in the South Pacific. On the
island of Tahiti he saw several natives weaving a
kind of mat from palm fronds which they then
dipped into a tub of hot tar. When the tar cooled
they tied this creation onto their feet and entered
the water. Owen was fascinated by the tremendous increase in speed that the natives were able
to produce using these "fins" in the ocean. That
same year he brought the idea back with him to
the States and began development of the first rubber swim fin.

In 1940 the swim fin was made available to the
public. For the Pinders, Jack, Wally and Charlie
it was a gift from King Neptune himself. As the
face mask revealed the undersea world to the eyes
of man, the swim fin now made that world accessible.

Jack recalls, "I first saw the fin in a movie news-
reel. They showed this fellow swimming by everyone else on the surface, and I thought, hey, this
might work even better underwater. It took me a
while to find a pair, but finally this sporting goods
store found them for me and I went immediately
down to the beach to try them out. I couldn't be-

lieve it—this was the first time I heard the water whistling by my ears. I had swum out to the middle of the cove before I realized it. Then I made my first dive and damn near ricocheted off the twenty-foot bottom."

Almost overnight the hunters moved farther away from the shoreline and closer to the blue edge. But the timing was poor; war was in full scale in Europe and about to break out worldwide. Just after Jack won San Diego's ocean paddleboard race for the year 1940, beach activities for most of civilization came to a standstill.

Diving was restricted to the occasional beach dive for the next four years. Jack spent the time attempting to develop a spear that could handle the large grouper waiting at Boomer Beach. Over the course of the war he created the detachable spear point that was to be used on the end of the spear pole. (Jack's design became the standard by which all other spear points were subsequently made.) Still, the major problem was power: how could he propel the spear point with enough force to penetrate the tough hide of the broomtail?

Jack's options were limited to available materials and his ability to fabricate. What seemed to be the logical step at that time was somehow to use a live cartridge to drive a detachable spearhead into the fish. Jack began to experiment with the idea of using a 38 caliber cartridge. At the time no civilian had any information on the effects of cartridge detonating underwater. Doctors cautioned him that the concussion could blow out his eardrums and perhaps injure him in other ways they couldn't predict. Going against the wishes of his wife and friends, Jack went ahead with his testing and suffered no ill effects from the discharging cartridges. (Several decades later the bangstick appeared, using the same principle and design as Jack's original power head.)

On September 11, 1945, armed with his powerhead spear pole and a retrieval system consisting of several hundred feet of clothesline. Jack entered the waters of Boomer Beach and shortly landed a one hundred and eighty-five-pound broomtail grouper, the first blue water fish ever taken in the Pacific by a free diving spearfisherman.

Soon after the war spearfishing became popular in those countries whose borders touched a large body of diveable water. Divers in England, France, Italy, Spain, Australia, and the United States were particularly enthusiastic.

Interestingly, spearfishing grew in different directions depending on the geographical locations of the hunting grounds. Florida and the islands of the Caribbean had the best of it; clear water and a prolific fish population produced the best underwater hunting in the world. But there was also an abundance of sharks in those waters and their aggressiveness kept many divers close to the Florida shores.

Except of course, the Pinders, who, now that the war was over, were able to take their eighteen-foot open boat across the Gulf Stream to the Bahamas. The territory was wide open: in the reefs in front of Bimini they pulled out grouper, hog fish, and snapper. Fred was the big workhorse, Don was slick as a seal, and young Art was a short step behind the two best spearfishermen in the United States. The three worked the Bahamas from West End to the Berry islands off Nassau, diving to depths of eighty feet and using their Hawaiian slings with pinpoint accuracy. Fish of gigantic proportions were being landed and with the abundant game available it took only a few years before the Pinders became legendary throughout the Bahamas.

The development of the speargun more or less controlled the progress of the Pacific hunter. The powerhead spear pole of Jack's, although effective for grouper, was limited in its capacity. Inspired by an Italian spring loaded speargun that Jack and Wally had seen several years earlier, the two built a rubber powered speargun and attached Jack's power head to it. With this new hunting tool and a container attached to hold the retrieval line, Jack and Wally were more inclined to look for larger game in the deeper waters outside the kelp beds.

In Los Angeles barely a hundred miles north, the pole spear now had a rubber sling at its base and was predominantly used along the shoreline for smaller fish.

By 1948 the Pinders were in top form, and to emphasize the point, Art, who was then nineteen years old, pulled off one of the great feats in blue water hunting.

"I was diving with Jasper Williams in deep water by Fowey rock off Cape Florida. We were looking for grouper and I felt this presence behind me. I whirled around and there was this huge sailfish (a hundred pounder) following me. In the same motion of my turn I pulled back the sling and shot the fish in the backbone, paralyzing it. I towed it back to the boat and as I heaved it in, the

arrow fell out and the fish came to life. It went
crazy in the boat, breaking up gear, flipping seats,
gas cans and Jasper over the side. The sailfish
almost made it over the side itself and I thought,
if I don't do something quickly, it's going to get
away and no one in the world is ever going to believe what happened. So I climbed into the boat
and threw myself down on the fish and rode it for
about ten minutes until it settled down enough
for Jasper to get a line around its tail and secure
it." (To give Art's achievement some perspective,
it wasn't until twenty-five years later, using a
three band speargun with a retrieval system, that
another sailfish was landed.)

The only divers close to the Pinder's accomplishments in the Bahamas were Jack, Wally and the
San Diego Bottom Scratchers, the first organized
spearfishing club in the United States, formed in
1933 by Jack, Glenn Orr and Ben Stone.

The San Diego divers had completed their final stretch from Boomer Beach to the outer edges
of the kelp bed fringing the deep La Jolla Canyon. Sharks moved up through the canyon on occasion, usually in small numbers, but what they
lacked in quantity they made up for in size; large
hammerheads made their appearance, and the aggressive duskys and the great white, which had
yet to achieve its fearsome reputation from the
movies.

The sharks did not deter Jack or Wally from
diving the canyon where they stalked the yellowtail and the elusive white sea bass. One morning
in the summer while Art speared his sailfish,
Wally almost drowned trying to land a large yellowtail off these beds. He had speared the fish

using Jack's power head, but the forty-pound fish had worked its way off the spearpoint. It was severely wounded so could not swim away quickly. Wally grabbed it and started to wrestle the fish up to the surface by hand. When he neared the top the fish took off toward the bottom, pulling Wally down with it. The yellow wrenched itself loose and Wally swam after it and got hold of it, then started again for the surface. Jack was on top resting on his paddleboard, having watched his partner make his initial dive. He was waiting for Wally to return to the surface and had no idea what was taking place beneath him. Wally, knowing his time was critically short, made one last effort to pull the fish to the surface. Along the way he passed out.

"I knew something was wrong," Jack said later, "but I didn't know where to begin to look. Then a short distance away, Wally floated to the surface, face down in the water. I really thought he was dead. I pulled him up on board and started beating on his back and damn if he didn't come around."

I remember reading about Wally's duel with the yellowtail and I suspect that that story was the beginning of the Bottom Scratchers' own extraordinary history in the Pacific. They captured the imagination of divers up and down the California coast. It was real life adventure taking place, not in the wilds of Africa, but right here in our own backyard.

By 1950 Cousteau's Aqua Lung became available to the public and the hunters were the first consumers to try this new underwater breathing device in the ocean. They were not overwhelmed by

the aqua lung and treated it more as a novelty
than as a revolutionary tool for man in the undersea world. Its bulkiness restricted free movement,
and the noise from the bubbles spooked the fish.
They preferred the quick easy movements of free
diving and could spear more fish without the lung
than with it, so it remained on the sidelines to be
used in the winter when the hunting was slow or
the visibility poor. The ocean was a free divers'
domain in the fifties and remained so until the
early sixties.

During the fifties spearfishing reached its ze-
nith in popularity. It was a new exciting sport.
Thrill seekers, athletes, and would-be adventur-
ers all pushed their way into diving and some
great hunters emerged. From Florida came Don
del Monico, Jack Kerns and Charlie Andrews, and
from California came Dick Jappe, Del Wren, Doc
Mathison, Big Jim Christenson, Paul Hoss, Ron
Merker, and a boat load of others.

The spearfishermen held their first National
Championships in the summer of 1950 at Laguna
Beach, California. The term "National" was loosely
used: the Florida divers never heard a word about
the meet, an oversight that started a rivalry between the California and Florida spearfishermen
that has lasted to this day. The team National
Champions invariably came from one of these two
groups; the winners almost always come from the
area where the meets are held. Neither group can
beat the other in its home territory.

The Pacific fathers participated in several national meets, but for many of them it was just a
bonus, a way of receiving recognition for what
they loved to do. In those early days the

spearfisherman was considered a bona fide athlete. In California the prestigious Helms Foundation, which awarded trophies to outstanding amateur athletes in various fields of sport, included Spearfisherman of the Year in their annual presentations. With strong support from the manufacturers of diving equipment, and continued recognition through *Skin Diver Magazine*, interest in the sport grew and the competitions became stronger with each new season.

The competitions not only raised the skill level of the divers, but also pushed them out into deeper water where they became increasingly aware of the large pelagics roaming on the outside. By 1952 the Arbalete and other spearguns from Europe were replacing the pole spear. Attempts were made to land white sea bass and yellowtail, but the spearguns were not powerful enough nor properly rigged, so the fish were usually lost, often taking the speargun with them.

Despite the Pinders' and the Bottom Scratchers' early breakthroughs, blue water hunting was new to the majority of free divers. They had no idea what they were up against on that great blue plain. Every dive was an adventure into the unknown, either with the creatures, the dive equipment, or with the hunter himself.

Paul Hoss recalls his first trip to La Paz in Baja California, Mexico, with Mel Fisher, who later discovered the treasure-filled Spanish galleon *Nuestra Señora de Atocha* in the Caribbean.

"We flew down to try out my new Arbalete speargun and Mel's newly built underwater housing for a movie camera. Mel thought he could make an underwater adventure film for possible sale in the United States. The sharks were everywhere in the gulf in those days and the Mexicans stood on our boat smiling as we jumped willingly into their infested waters.

"Mel is looking for some hot footage and suggests to me that I spear this fair sized manta ray that is flying beneath the boat. I have no idea what a manta can do, so I drop down and pull off on the big ray. The lightweight spear bounces off its hide and wraps around one of the horns and the manta takes off with a full head of steam, pulling me and gun down so fast that I almost drown before the line untangles and frees up the gun."

"Mel complains that 'It all happened too fast. Try it again,' I know better and refuse."

" 'All right,' says Mel, "then you better shoot this shark that is coming up beneath us.' I agreed, but only out of necessity, and spear the shark as it cuts by closely. The shark takes off with a force that pulls my face mask off, then my fins and finally strips the gun out of my hand, all in a matter of seconds."

"Mel complains again, 'Still too fast. One more time.'"

But there is no mask, no fins and no gun. In mid-morning of the first day, the great La Paz hunt and underwater film spectacular comes to a premature end.

The divers' ignorance of the strength and power of the ocean creatures was equal to their lack of understanding of the general physics of diving. It was assumed and accepted that to free dive meant to endure tremendous pain in the ears. The divers knew nothing about equalizing the middle ear pressure with the outside water pressure by holding their nose and blowing, forcing air back up the eustachian tubes and into the middle ear. Instead, they ate the pain. Naturally, over the years they developed severe middle ear problems, and today most have hearing difficulties and must rely on hearing aids and a good deal of shouting when they get among each other.

The aqua lung also appeared with an equally appalling lack of information. When Paul Hoss acquired his "lung" in 1953, he was pleased to find that by holding his breath at every opportunity he could make an hour bottle last over two hours.

"Oh, I'd spit up a little blood every now and then, but I wrote that off as the result of breathing compressed air."

So it went. Mistakes were made, sometimes serious ones, and the Ocean in its direct way was teaching man how to operate within its realm.

Up until 1956-7, the Los Angeles divers had been content with the European spearguns that were designed for fish under twenty pounds. They had heard what the Bottom Scratchers were up to in San Diego and several unsuccessful attempts were made to get hold of one of Jack's guns. One Saturday afternoon Paul went down to San Diego "just to take a look."

Having continually refined the rubber powered speargun which he and Wally had designed, the San Diego speargun could hold three hundred pounds of pressure from the rubber slings, and the trigger mechanism could release it as smooth as butter. (Jack's design was later copied and used in the first commercial speargun marketed by the U.S. firm Swim Master.)

Paul's eye went over every centimeter of the

trigger mechanism and he returned to Los Angeles and simply duplicated it. The next ten years,
into the early 60's, Paul became the primary
builder of blue water spearguns in Los Angeles.

The divers in Los Angeles were ready for a blue
water gun. They had seen the dazzling schools of
whites and yellows along the outside, and like the
Pinders and the Bottom Scratchers, they were
drawn to the challenge. With Paul's speargun in
hand they moved out of the kelp beds and drifted
into blue water country.

At this point many older divers who had never
cared much for the competitions, abandoned them,
"...preferring," as Big Jim Christenson put it, "the
blue water where competition's meaningless; out
there it's just you and the fish. Let the young ones
compete."

The second generation of spearfishermen who
had been standing in the shadow of their pioneer-
ing fathers finally took their turn on stage. They
had been preparing for this moment through years
of "B" competitions. In truth, their stalking skills
with the smaller fish were equal to those of the
older divers and they were decidedly more aggressive in the water. The second generation took
what the first had given them, refining their hunting skills to an art form, and producing some outstanding divers: Terry Lentz, Jay Riffe, Jim
Baldwin, Mike Wilkie, later followed by Al
Scheneppershoff, Bob Donnell, Mike Oceanus, Bob
Stanbery, Don Evers, Yas Ikeda and a dozen more.
Terry Lentz became the only American ever to win
an individual World's championship in interna-
tional competitive spearfishing. (On the island of
Malta in the Mediterranean, no less. These cham-

pionships are nearly always won by members of the host country because they know the territory better than any visitor could possibly know it in the short time he is there.)

In the early 60's the face of diving began to change rapidly. The Aqua Lung was now called SCUBA and Cousteau's film, *The Silent World* had turned the nation on to a recreation that was immediate and available to everyone. The masses were suiting up and putting on a SCUBA rig that did not require years of free diving experience to be able to function effectively underwater.

The SCUBA technology, with its tremendous appeal, steamrolled over the free divers and their art of spearfishing. The annual awards stopped coming, the manufacturers withdrew their support of the competitions and *Skin Diver Magazine* shifted with the SCUBA trend. In a matter of a few years, the men who had forged the path to the undersea world were forgotten.

As the tribe slipped into obscurity the second generation of Pacific hunters, perhaps frustrated by the sudden turn of events, became fiercely determined to hold on to their heritage and shine in a light of their own making. But they, like the fathers before them, needed a new territory to conquer, a place where they could strike out in bold fashion and make their history. During the 60's they found what they were looking for in the Sea of Cortez, Mexico. The Gulf of California, as it's sometimes called, is less than a hundred miles from the California/Arizona border. From its most northern tip this body of water stretches 1,100 miles south to Cabo San Lucas where it meets with the Pacific. Only a hundred miles wide at its broadest point, the Gulf, as the hunters came to call it, held more game fish per square foot of water than any territory yet discovered.

4

THE GULF

Prior to the 60's the Gulf of California and the land surrounding it, particularly its western shore, the Baja peninsula, were as much a wilderness as any of the unsettled regions of Africa during that same period. The volcanic terrain of Baja California, brutally rugged, made the Gulf virtually inaccessible to the outside world, thus keeping its pristine beauty and teeming waters primordially intact.

The few Americans who did reach the Gulf were generally fishermen who flew in on private planes and only they and the Mexicans born to the Gulf ever managed to land the grouper, *pez fuerte* (amberjack), dorado, pargo (snapper), rooster fish, wahoo, tuna and totuava (white sea bass), that schooled in this wild spit of salt water. The Mexican fishing fleet, what there was of it, were shrimpers and bottom dredgers, and did not fish for the grouper and other large free swimming fish. It was too expensive to use gill nets on these strong fish because they would tear up a good net that was often irreplaceable. So the Mexican fishermen used their nets on smaller fish and left the big ones for the hand line and the occasional fishing rod.

Traveling down the thousand-mile peninsula was unthinkable without a durable four-wheel-drive vehicle. There were no paved roads and the dirt roads were treacherous, often becoming riverbed where the land dictated. The one road that could be traveled to the Gulf was the road to Guaymas on the mainland of Mexico. It ran down the western border of Mexico along the eastern shore of the Gulf, past Kino Bay through Hermosillo, down to San Carlos Bay then into Guaymas and beyond. It was in these two bays, Kino and San Carlos, that the second generation of divers first launched their boats.

Diving the Gulf during this period was a perilous undertaking because equal to the abundant fish population was a proportionate number of sharks. When a fish was speared it would call out to not one or two sharks, but to a half dozen or more that would converge on the area and compete with the diver for the struggling fish, the man often losing the battle as the shark would take the easy meal before the fish could be boated. Although there was considerable contact with sharks that often left the hunters jumpy, no one was ever bitten.

When the hunters began to work Kino Bay and San Carlos they found that the gear used to hunt the yellowtail and white sea bass in the Pacific could not hold up to the powerful fish in the gulf.

A medium sized grouper (fifty pounds) would destroy a steel arrow, bending it into impossible shapes; the fish would snap cable, break shooting line, and crack off the metal spear heads attached to the arrows. A large *pez* would sound with unstoppable power, stripping all the line off a reel in the blink of an eye, then pull the gun and diver down until, unable to turn the fish, the man would have to let go of his rig or drown. Large pargo would respond like the grouper, tearing through the rocks and ledges in an attempt to break the line attached to the arrow, and doing it more often than not. The hunters were not prepared for what the fish, particularly the grouper, could do to their equipment.

They returned from the Gulf with outlandish tales, their broken gear providing proof to the disbelieving. Jack and Wally in San Diego and in Los Angeles, Charlie, who had now begun to design and fabricate blue water equipment, would examine the rubble, see where it had broken down then redesign and construct new gear that might stand the test.

By the late 60's, major changes had taken place in the Gulf. There had developed a world market for shark livers and the Mexican fishermen longlined the easily catchable sharks into a minority, except for the very large ones which they feared would sink their boats, and which remain to this day the guardians of those waters.

In addition to the reduced shark population, new roads and stronger off road vehicles made reachable formerly inaccessible areas. The tribe, now allowed to travel the previously forbidden lands and dive in virgin waters, began to explore the Baja Peninsula with enthusiastic determination. The gear developed by Jack, Wally and Charlie was holding up to the fish, and refined hunting techniques were putting fish in the boat that before had been lost. It was during this period that I was christened by the waters of the Gulf.

I barely knew Sam and Leo, a couple of renegade hunters who had been diving the gulf for years. They needed a third person to share in the expenses and it was only by chance that I happened to be available. We rented a single engine plane and flew twelve hundred miles south to the very tip of Baja, Cabo San Lucas. After an eleven-hour flight, we landed on a dirt runway as Leo finished his story about a fatal plane crash that had occurred on this same runway the last time he and Sam were there. After parking the plane, we walked fifty yards to the beach and set up camp next to the little cannery. The following morning we suited up and swam out into placid clear water directly in front of our campsite. Thirty yards from shore the bottom drops off into a deep underwater canyon up which the *pez* swim, looking for the bait which drift close to the pilings of the cannery and feed on its refuse.

Having no idea how to stalk the fish, I watch Sam and Leo make their drops into the transparent water, then copy their moves. They soon swim out into deeper water and I remain close to the edge of the dropoff. Within ten minutes a school of *pez* glide in and I dive down on my first blue water game fish. The *pez* ooze raw power in their barely discernible movements. Their eyes are large and their streamlined bodies glisten amber.

They reflect a fearlessness in their body attitude as they angle toward me for a closer look. I line up on the smallest of the four and release the arrow. The fish immediately sounds with a fury that is startling. Grabbing the line which is zipping off of the reel, I feel for the first time the impressive strength of an open water fish. By Gulf standards the amberjack is small, maybe twenty pounds, yet I must kick hard to keep the battle even. It's difficult to believe that so much power can be packaged in a fish that is no longer than my leg. On the surface my additional buoyancy wears the fish down and after five minutes of hauling on the line I'm able to pull it to the surface. When it reaches my hand I feel as though I have scaled the highest peak on a far mountain range that before I could only admire from the foothills.

Each morning for a week we dive the canyon and I support my euphoria with one fish a day, each one larger than the last. At noon we take our fish to a small restaurant/house run by a Mexican woman and trade it for a wonderful lunch and grand dinner. Then at night we lie on the beach and watch shooting stars in the crystalline sky. I could have lived that way forever.

Spearfishing was the central reason for coming to Baja, but it shortly became for me a secondary attraction to the incomparable setting of the Gulf. Never had I imagined such a place. There were as many birds in the sky as fish in the sea: terns by the thousands, gulls of several varieties flying in packed flocks, pelicans gliding in tight formations and stretching in lines for fifty miles or more, albatross and frigates floating on steady wings high in the invisible thermoclines. Even the osprey

appears, circling her fortress of a nest built on
the exposed outcrop of a high cliff. The air and
sea pulsate with more life than I thought could
exist in one place. Standing in mute contrast are
the primordial volcanic mountains that lie
stripped of vegetation in colors of red rust and
chalky granite, the colors vibrating against the
blinding blue of the Baja sky.

As I settled into the life of a blue water hunter,
the week ended. The following Monday it was back
to work, walled inside a windowless office with a
restless discontent that would not leave me. Something had happened in Mexico. I thought that it
might have been the first thrill of spearing a big
fish, though in truth I knew it to be the place itself. That untamed country, distant and untouched
by civilized man, felt strangely familiar, and
tapped the center of my soul.

Seven months later, I made a second trip to the
Gulf, this time by car to San Carlos bay. There I
met some of the reigning chiefs of the second generation: Jay Riffe, Al Schneppershoff, Bob Donnell,
Jim Watt, Bob Stanbery, Yas Ikeda and a dozen
more from the spearfishing club The Long Beach
Neptunes. There was a dive meet with an Arizona
club in progress. Their mood was serious, so I had
no chance to dive with them, although I and another newcomer joined several divers in a boat
ride and were dropped off in water somewhat removed from the deep water reefs they planned to
work. When they returned several hours later the
boat was filled with fish. Some were of enormous
size, as big around as a football player and five to
six feet in length; all were grouper. It did not seem
physically possible that a man could single-

handedly land such fish on a breath hold. I knew it could be done, I'd seen pictures, but the physical reality of these fish gave a different perspective and made their feats all the more astounding. Sitting in the boat as it headed back to San Carlos, I listened to the divers talk about the fish and the water, and by the time we rounded the mouth of the bay I had decided to throw in with this group and be a part of the adventure that lay waiting here.

Eight months later in the fall of that same year, my opportunity came. While in San Carlos I obtained the names and numbers of several of the Long Beach Neptunes and had kept in contact with them. Word reached me that Frank Taylor of San Diego was putting a trip together and I gave him a call. He said he was going to trailer his eighteen-foot Glaspar down to San Felipe, the most northern town inside the gulf, then make a ninety-mile run by water to Gonzaga Bay. There we would rendezvous with other divers and hunt what is called the midriff; a series of small islands east of Gonzaga.

"Are you interested?"

"Definitely."

"Welcome aboard."

There are never any guarantees when traveling into the Gulf. Many of the subsequent trips I took were blown out by wind, or the water conditions were too poor to dive, or the boat broke down, or the car broke down, or the roads washed out. Every calamity that could occur did, but this trip to Gonzaga was different; it had the magic of the beginner's voyage.

Towing Frank's boat from San Diego to the town

of San Felipe takes a full day on the only paved
road in the Gulf that lies west of the mainland.
Upon arriving we eat dinner, then Frank, Jack
Pesh, and I sleep in the boat on its trailer for the
night. At 6 AM we wake to a hot windless morning
and breakfast in a small cantina, then launch the
Osprey at nine—high tide. We begin the nearly
hundred-mile stretch at full throttle, skimming
our way down the Gulf on a rippleless blue-green
carpet. The inviting sea is in sharp opposition to
the rugged, uninhabitable land, and I wonder
about the men we are to meet, who must make
their way to Gonzaga by dirt road and trail. In
two and a half hours the outlines of the midriff
islands appear and Frank steers for the largest.
In the last hour we are accompanied by a sizeable
school of porpoise who play their game of high
speed tag just under the bow of the *Osprey*.

The ideal conditions allow us to make the islands in a record three and a half hours. We are
far ahead of schedule, so have time for a two-hour
drive before going into Gonzaga. Frank pulls into
the west end of the island called Salvatierra and
Jack lowers the anchor near an area where Frank
had seen grouper on his last trip down. We suit
up, Frank and Jack swim east and I swim off in
the opposite direction. Having hunted for grouper only once before in San Carlos, I know very
little other than that the fish like a sandy bottom
that is strewn with large boulders.

The thirty-foot visibility is not nearly as clear
as it was in San Carlos or at the Cape. In fact it
borders on dirty, much like the Pacific sometimes
is in the summer, when residue hangs in the water like dust. I drop down to a rocky slope twenty

feet deep that slants away to a bottom that is not
visible. Taking it slowly and feeling my way along,
I try to dive deeper with each new breath hold. In
thirty minutes I find my limit at forty feet. Diving to a boulder and remaining motionless, I remember the advice I received in San Carlos. "Move
slowly: let the grouper come to you." Following
those instructions and continuing west around the
island, I move from one promising boulder to the
next. Another ten minutes pass and I'm down half
hidden behind a boulder, watching a dark shape
take form to my right in deeper water—a grouper making its way toward me. The speargun is
lying straight out on top of the boulder and the
grouper continues to swim until it is eight feet
away and directly in front of the speargun. When
the fish turns broadside I pull the trigger. The
arrow strikes the fish dead center and it powers
off down the steep slope toward the bottom. Holding the line in an attempt to work against it, I am
pulled down with unexpected power. The line suddenly stops running and I quickly swim for the
surface. Not quite sure of my next step, it seems
reasonable to me to begin hauling in the line. After a hitch or two and with surprising ease, I'm
able to pull the fish to the surface. There is no
further struggle and I grip the narrow space below its gills and swim back to the *Osprey*. Frank
is in the boat and as I hand the fish up to him
says, in a half joking manner, "Keep those little
ones in the water until they grow up some." The
fish is larger than the biggest amberjack I'd
speared at the Cape, and his comment dissolves
my elation. Stoically, I ask for my other speargun
and return to the same area.

After twenty minutes my dives have inched their way down to forty-five feet. At that depth, the bottom is darkly visible twenty-five feet below. This new area is filled with colorful tropical fish. Distracted by their flutterings I do not immediately see the black shape rising out of the bottom. When I see it, everything stops: time, my heart, my thoughts. The fish is larger than a man, or so it appears; its head alone looks larger than the full body of the last grouper. All my confidence is suddenly gone. Slowly, the grouper moves toward me. The speargun tracks it with equal slowness. When the great fish is within ten feet of the end of the arrow, it turns and offers its broadsides.

Someone else pulls the trigger and neither he nor I have any notion as to what will happen next. The fish explodes down the slope with awesome force; the line is moving off the reel so fast that it cannot keep pace and I'm being dragged down into deeper water. Several seconds later the fish stops running and I turn and pump for the surface, out of breath, speargun in hand, line rolling off the reel. Pushing hard, the ascent becomes a sprint for breath. Bursting through the top, my heart pounds with excitement, echoing my gasping breaths.

I'm neither comfortable nor sure what to do next. While regaining my wind I gather up the slack line so there is a direct route down to the fish beneath me. Kicking furiously and pulling hard on the line, I try to hoist the fish to the surface as I did the last grouper, but it comes to nothing; I might as well try to pull up a pier piling. While breathing deeply and attempting to regain a clear head, the thought runs through me that I

am engaged in the oldest struggle since man began to hunt for his food. This is a direct and inti-
mate duel between man and animal that has been
reduced to the physical level. I've no advantage
as the hunter in this environment.

I've settled down enough, after five minutes of
steady breathing, to attempt a dive. Filling my
lungs, I take one last breath to capacity and drop
down the line. Pulling myself hand over hand I
descend beyond my own depth limit to around
fifty-five feet. The line runs into a cave which has
a three-foot opening. The end of my arrow appears
in the upper portion of the entrance. Holding on
to the arrow, I give it a pull. Nothing happens, no
movement. Pulling hard stirs the fish. Then putting my finned feet next to the opening for lever-
age I pull down and out. The fish releases from
the cave and I fall over backward, out of breath.
The grouper is enormous, still alive, but spent.
With nothing left in me and needing air badly I
push off the bottom toward the surface, which is
now light years away. The same instincts guide
the grouper into deeper water. Watching it and
knowing that if it holes up farther down I'll never
be able to retrieve it, I snatch the line and continue to kick for the surface. Halfway up, I'm
brought to a halt; the line connecting me to the
fish is bow string tight and both the fish and I are
suspended in the water swimming, but moving
nowhere. We hold the moment for a few seconds,
but I'm running on empty and can go no further.
As I'm about to release the line the fish gives a
little, then it gives some more and we're moving
toward the surface again. Straining for the ceiling, the panic of drowning lodges in my throat and

I wonder if they will find me if I pass out. Breaking through the surface, my head is dizzy and flashes of light bounce around the inside of my skull. Completely limp from the effort, my legs and arms tingle as I heave new life into my oxygen-depleted body.

Sitting slouched in the boat and staring at the single fish filling the section between the gas tanks and the rear seat, it is difficult for me to believe that I have taken this fish as I have. Remembering the strong impressions I had of that boat load of fish in San Carlos and the seemingly impossible deeds of those divers, I try to put this grouper into some kind of perspective, but I can't. After having landed such a fish I'm no closer to explaining how it's done.

Frank and Jack are out of sight and are probably struggling with their own fish. I've no desire, no strength to spear another fish. But wanting to get as much feel for this new water as possible, I restring the speargun and fit another steel arrow—the last is bent beyond repair—and return to the water.

Swimming in the Gulf is like swimming in an overstocked aquarium: the food chain becomes visible in these waters. Clouds of nearly transparent minute fish swim just under the surface; beneath them schools of silver and blue bait fish meander, below, the cabrillo, the sierra mackerel and the other free swimming predators, and in the depths rest the lords of this territory, the grouper.

A school of fast moving yellowtail swim by, and I dive down on them with absolutely no idea how to draw the yellows in. They barely give me a look before moving off. While hanging motionless in mid-water, I see another school of yellows and this time they swing by me. I snap off a quick shot and to my amazement, hit one. It is strong for its slender size, but after the grouper I waste no time hauling it in. Swimming back to the boat I see that Jack and Frank are on board looking over the big grouper. Handing the yellow up to Frank I climb aboard, anxious to see what fish they have brought in, but mine are the only fish in the boat. Frank says he has seen a few fish, but could not get deep enough for a good shot. My beginner's luck seems to be at work, and I say nothing for fear of breaking the spell.

Pulling anchor we head for Gonzaga Bay and within forty minutes are idling into Papa Fernandez settlement. On shore waiting to greet us are nine men. Some I recognize from San Carlos, others I know only by reputation.

During the mid-sixties an underwater romantic, Hank Holcomb, published a newspaper called *Pacific Underwater News*. Hank was convinced that diving needed some additional stimulation, something that might pump further interest into the sport. His paper focused on spearfishing and blue water hunting, a courageous idea in view of the fall spearfishing had taken in the last five years. The paper was distributed to the dive shops on a regular basis, and issues became my first link with the group which in part stands before me. Each month the names and pictures of Al Schneppershoff, Mike Oceanus, Bob Donnell, Don Evers, Yas Ikeda, Bob Stanbery and others would appear on the pages of Hank's paper. The clans of the other California divers were also featured.

San Diego had their second generation of blue water hunters who followed in the footsteps of Jack and Wally. Northern California had its group. But it was the Los Angeles bunch that formed the nucleus for the majority of the stories. From this group, Al stood out as the hunter who always seemed to land the big fish of the season. He became a cult hero of sorts and Hank kept him in the headlines until the paper folded in the 70's. Now they are here in Gonzaga, slipped from the pages of the News: Al, Bob Donnell, Mike, Bob Stanbery, and from San Carlos, Larry Brakovitch and John Lockridge.

As the boat is unloaded and the fish are brought ashore, everyone's attention is on the big grouper. When it is learned that all the fish are mine, the men immediately accept me as a hunter worthy of their clan. The comradeship that was absent in San Carlos comes to life here in Gonzaga. Making no mention of my mysterious run of luck, I accept their acknowledgments with equanimity of a seasoned hunter.

This river of good fortune now has pushed me into that rare current where dream is merged with reality. Through the gathering walks an older Mexican with a small boy clinging to his hand. The man asks me if he can have a fish for his family. Delighted with the request, I gave him both the small grouper and the yellowtail, and the river keeps right on rolling. Larry fillets out the big grouper and lays wire mesh over a smoldering campfire. In an hour we are all sitting down to barbecued grouper, ears of corn and baked potatoes.

During the meal stories of big fish and wild

times spread around the open fire, often inter-
rupted with burst of laughter when the stories
become outlandish. There is no need for exaggera-
tion. The truth borders on the unbelievable. The
conversation turns to tomorrow; everyone is anxious to dive and seem fired up by my big grouper.
With a full day before us, the feast breaks up an
hour after the sun has gone down and I slip into
my sleeping bag exhausted, and fall asleep instantly.

Frank wakes me the next morning. The sky is
still dark and barely hints of sunrise in the east.
Someone's building a fire and the divers are bus-
tling about, eating breakfast and getting their
gear in order. The mood is quiet and deliberate, a
contrast from last night. The seriousness snaps
me alert. My gear is already in the boat so I sit
and drink hot chocolate, watching the others break
in the day. The sun sets the horizon ablaze and a
Baja masterpiece is mirrored in the glassy bay.
Shortly after sunrise two boats, each loaded with
gear and half a dozen divers, head directly into
the heart of a sun that is rising out of the mouth
of the bay. Once outside in the open water the two
boats separate and the one with Al, Bob Stanbery,
Jack Pesch and the others heads north. Frank's
boat with Bob Donnell, Mike, John, Larry and me
continues east. I've no idea where we are going,
nor enough curiosity to ask; it is the expectation
of things to come that has me in it its grip. All
divers are silent, bending in unison to absorb the
shock of the plunging boat. The *Osprey*'s bow
points to a sheer-walled volcanic island that rises
out of the water in the distance. I am strangely
empty of thought and stare blankly at the island

as though I am about to enter an unknowable world for which I have no experience or understanding.

A forty-minute boat ride puts us on the south side of Puma island. The *Osprey* will drop a team of two divers every quarter mile along the length of the island. The last team in the boat will anchor, then enter the water. The team that is dropped off before the boat is anchored will eventually arrive, pull anchor then swing back to pick up the others and ahead to retrieve the remaining two. Then we move farther up the island and begin again in new territory.

My partner is Bob Donnell, an outstanding diver, who several years later became National Spearfishing Champion. We are the second team, and jump off near the middle of Puma, where the cliffs drop vertically into the water and continue straight down fifty feet to a sandy, boulder-ridden bottom. The visibility is much improved over yesterday—now close to fifty feet—giving me a clear view of Bob's dives as I watch him from the surface. Using no more than the fewest possible kicks, he breaks into a glide that sends him to the bottom where he settles behind a boulder and waits. In thirty seconds he lifts from the boulder and moves half hidden to another, twenty-five feet ahead, and waits. When no fish appear, he moves another twenty-five feet. In roughly a minute and a half he gently ascends from his position, disturbing nothing in the process, and kicks his way to the surface.

Blue water hunting is learned by doing and the Gulf may well be the last place where an apprenticeship can be undertaken. There are no books,

films or cassettes of instruction on the stalking
techniques required to hunt in blue water. The
hunters themselves offer little in the way of instruction or encouragement. Bob is a rare exception. He shares his knowledge and observations
willingly. After watching my dives he tells me that
I tend to rush things, that I'm moving too quickly
along the bottom after my initial drop. He is right.
These dives are deeper than I am used to, making
me tense, and it is reflected in my short breath
hold which causes me to hurry the dive.

Up and down we work, making our way eastward. I have stayed in good physical condition by
running daily and diving often on the California
coast, but after forty minutes my legs are beginning to lose their snap. We cover our quarter mile
and I'm glad for the rest when the *Osprey* picks
us up.

Fifteen minutes later we are back in the water,
dropped into a section nearer the eastern tip, the
farthest extension of the island into the Gulf.
There is a current running and we have to pick
up our kick or risk being carried out past the island and into the mainstream of the Gulf. This continual kicking uses energy and it digs into my
bottom time. The extra work has no visible effect
on Bob, who maintains his same pace, moving easily to the depths and back. At the island's end a
school of large yellowtail cruises by twenty feet
beneath me. Bob is already down and spears one.
While working the fish, he looks up and motions
me down. I dive to his depth where the yellows
are circling Bob and the speared fish, drawn to
its gyrating movements. Aiming carefully, I release
the arrow and the shot catches the backbone of

one of the fish, killing it instantly. The boat has moved up and around the island and there is no place to put our fish, so we string them to our weight belts. Swimming in these waters with a bloody fish tied to my body is more than a little disconcerting, and I divide my attention between diving, watching Bob, and looking for sharks. Bob continues to make the same runs with the same efficiency and is unaffected by the possibilities that are abundantly clear to me.

Bob's dives are a study in economy, never using more energy than he needs and utilizing maximum effectiveness from each breath hold. He exudes confidence and a complete sense of freedom in the water. His dives are so strong that the idea of risk seems absurd. One might just as well ask if it is risky for a seal to hunt in the ocean. I, on the other hand, cannot share his confidence and continue to keep a sharp eye out for sharks.

Soon, and to my relief, we are picked up by the *Osprey* and swing around to work the north side of the island. After several hours of diving we have covered the entire circumference of Puma. No one has seen grouper. We have dived hard and have only the yellowtail to show for a full morning's work. In the early afternoon we discover a pinnacle barely breaking water several miles north of Puma out in the open water. It is a new location. No one has seen it before. John jumps in to give it a quick scout and after several dives, offers a thumbs up approval. The boat is anchored and the hunters spread out and away from one another to work the peripheries of the pinnacle which turns out to be the tip of an extensive underwater reef in sixty feet of water that is filled with grouper.

In thirty minutes I manage to spear two fish, neither as large as the one I speared the day before, but strong enough to destroy the last of my arrows. These long dives have worn me out and I would like to watch the others stalk, but the water here is deeper and I cannot see what is taking place beneath me. Bob returns from a long dive and has speared a big one. Exhausted from the dive, he asks if I will go down and pull it out. These last two days have given me an exaggerated sense of my abilities and caught up in the excitement, I agree to help. Pumping up long and deep, then dropping down the line, I follow it down to sixty feet, where the light is noticeably dimmer. The line runs into a large cave on the bottom. From the entrance I can make out the fish, which is ten feet or so inside and has pushed its head and upper body into a crevice and opened its gills, wedging itself between the rocks. Bob forewarned me of this possibility and instructed me to take hold of the gills and force them closed, then pull the fish out by its head. Moving to the head of the fish and wrapping my arms around the back of its head, which is larger than my chest, I close the gills and swim against the fish, pushing it out until it is free. The grouper is finished and makes no attempt to swim off. Completely out of breath, I push off for the surface. Halfway up, I realize I'll never make it to the top and use the line to help pull myself along. Bob, floating on the surface, senses what is happening and draws hard on the line pulling both the fish and me to the surface. I reach the top in much the same wrungout condition as I did yesterday and float weak and hollow on the surface, realizing how easy it is in these highly charged surroundings to go beyond my limits.

The hunters continue to bring fish to the boat. Frank has had a grouper hole up and cannot dislodge it. Bob, along with John and Larry, work the fish for twenty minutes before freeing it up. We have been on this pinnacle for several hours and weary divers are beginning to collect in the boat. I am one of the first.

The boat is low in the water with its cargo, and the men have nowhere to sit other than on the fish or the gunnels. There's too much weight in the boat for Frank to get it up on a plane. The wind is up and we take water over the bow. Someone tells a story of a Mexican skiff sinking from the weight of fish brought in by divers on another trip last year. Again I'm floating in that nether world between fantasy and reality, but this time I'm not alone. Everyone is grinning. Mike lets out a war whoop and each diver bellows out his own sound. He says, "There is nothing, anywhere, that compares to this." There is no argument, there is only exhilaration, and it glows on every face in the boat.

I wonder about the success of the other hunting party. I doubt they could have been as fortunate as we were. Rounding the mouth of Gonzaga Bay we head for Papa's settlement. The other boat is already in and Frank steers for it at full throttle, turning at the last instant to a chorus of hoots from both groups. The other boat is filled with fish. It's hard to believe that they could have had the same success, but with the divers it was carrying, I shouldn't be surprised; no one else seems to be.

We pull all the fish out of the boats and lay them on the rocky beach, where small wind waves lap the shore and keep the flies off of the fish as they are being cleaned. The children and the men of the settlement come down to the shore and admire the catch. There is a lot of meat here and I ask Bob Donnell what we are going to do with it all. He laughs and says, "Watch."

Then the knives of the hunters and the Mexicans come out and the butchering begins. Larry tells me there is no one faster or surer with the knife than a Mexican fisherman. They are indeed deft, but the hunters are no laggards themselves. In an hour, over fifteen hundred pounds of fish are cleaned. The Mexicans are offered to take what they can use and they take almost everything. What remains goes into our ice chests. The birds descend on the carcasses and efficiently pick them bare. What is left is eaten by the crabs that have descended on the remains as they sink beneath the wind waves. The Gulf provides and absorbs with equal efficiency.

Fires erupt into life around our camp. A fiesta is in the making. The sun disappears behind the volcanic mountain range in the west leaving us in twilight and the Mexicans return with tortillas, salsa and a pot of beans. The fish is put on the grill and the tequila has replaced the Mexican beer. Standing off to one side, I watch the festivities. The Mexicans speak no English and only Bob Donnell speaks Spanish, yet they all understand one another. Each group resides in the same time warp, a thousand years ago when man and nature were still connected at the belly.

The conversation of the hunters never strays

far from blue water, talking gear and fish and ask-
ing the Mexicans in pictures drawn in the dirt
where the big fish might be found further down
the Gulf. It is evident that whatever else these
men do when they are not in the water is just filling time until they can get back to it. Much of their
time is spent speculating on new territories that
often turn up empty when explored.

I don't know whether their enjoyment is in the
pursuit of virgin waters or the actual hunting of
the fish—probably a little of both.

Bob Donnell believes that motivation above all
else determines a blue water hunter. He says you
have to really want to do it, almost to the point of
obsession. "Why else would one be willing to drive
the Baja roads, encountering one ordeal after another just to reach some untried waters, or climb
out of a warm bunk before the sun has risen, to
put on a cold wet suit, then jump into the still
colder Pacific day after day, often seeing no fish
and receiving no reward for the effort. Motivation," says Bob, "is Al's greatest strength," and he
tells the story (that everyone but me has heard)
of the tribe getting together for an albacore hunt.

***

The albacore is a sleek bullet-like member of
the tuna family. It travels from fifty to several hundred miles off shore in the open ocean. The albacore is very difficult to spear because it continually swims at top speed, close to forty miles an
hour, and the hunter has only a split second to

line up into a blurred school before it disappears. "Well," Bob continues, "we set out in the wee hours of the morning in search for albacore and traveled all morning and into the early afternoon trolling for a school and listening to the radio for any hookups by other boats that would pinpoint the fish. By mid-afternoon we had come up empty and decided to head back to port. En route we cross a kelp paddy (a section of kelp which has broken away from the main bed and is floating unattached on the open sea). Still dressed in our street clothes, we look over the side and see a single yellowtail cruising in and out of the paddy. It is the only game fish we've seen in the last twelve hours. The boat circles for a better look and as it does one diver pulls out his gear, then everyone is shoving and pushing to get into their gear and be the first one in the water for the single yellowtail. The water is cold and the wet suit cumbersome to put on in the heavy sea. I've got one leg in my suit and look up to see Al, dressed in only his fins and mask and holding his speargun, jump over the side and into the water. Everybody hears the splash and the keystone cops act suddenly stops in mid-action. Everyone leans over the side of the boat to watch Al, naked, stalk and spear the fish, then bring it aboard to disbelieving laughter."

The evening is slipping away and a pleasant weariness sets in. The Mexicans are wandering back to their shacks and following their lead, I head for my sleeping bag. The conversation is still animated and I fall asleep listening to it from a distance.

There is a laziness to the morning. Those who

are up stumble in slow motion, either from
yesterday's diving or last night's celebration. My
body feels used and my legs are tight. The success of yesterday's hunt provides the Mexicans
with all the fish they need and without adequate
refrigeration for an additional catch, there is little
reason to go out today. That suits me. My enthusiasm (motivation?) is not there. Everyone else
looks a little fatigued as well. Al and Bob Stanbery
are the exceptions, and bounce down to their boat.
They want to make a morning dive. Mike goes with
them.

We will be going back tomorrow, so at Frank's
suggestion I hike up to the hill above the settlement to look at a Christ figure constructed from
automobile parts. With a panoramic view of the
Gulf before me, the artwork of a man is unimpres-
sive and I sit down to enjoy the Gulf's primordial
beauty. The water shimmers like a finely cut em-
erald, and the islands we dove yesterday sit low
in the water like rough brown stones carefully
placed. Far to the south lies Guardian Angel, like
a sleeping giant rising above all the other islands.
There has been only one expedition to Guardian
Angel. Frank was a member of that party. He
speaks about the island in mixed tones of rever-
ence and excitement. It is a paradise, with clear
water, enormous grouper, and sea turtles, and a
dense sea lion colony. Many different species of
big fish are said to school off of that mysterious
island. It is a hard journey to Guardian Angel. Its
nearest point from the peninsula is another seventy-five miles of horrendous dirt road, then fifty
miles of open water through a channel that can
be peaceful one moment and a raging gale the

next. There is no Coast Guard, no radio contact, no help of any kind.

Sitting on the hill, wondering if I will ever have the opportunity to dive Guardian Angel, I've no way of knowing that over the next fifteen years, I'll dive it on eight different occasions and travel the length and breadth of the Gulf many times, diving the majority of the islands from here to Cabo San Lucas. In these waters I'll encounter sharks, killer whales, and nearly every species of game fish that swims here. I'll dive with finback whales, pilot whales and gray whales, ride turtles and whale sharks. The fishermen in their remote camps up and down the Gulf will come to know me and I them and we will sit in mutual friendship. When the road goes in and stretches in an unbroken line the length of the peninsula, the Gulf will change; fishermen who used to gladly give us a boat for a day in exchange for our fish will charge as much as a hundred dollars a day for the same boat. Once hardy fishermen will become grasping rental agents. Empty coves next to fishing villages where we camped alone will be filled with cars, trucks, and RV's, and there will be men collecting money for parking. Tons of trash will accumulate and I'll watch as man turns this untamed stretch of land into another of his civilized disasters.

The waters of the Gulf will fare no better than the land. The big powerful game fish are gold to the American fisherman. In a decade empty waters will stand where once flourished large colonies of grouper. Guardian Angel will be wiped clean of grouper by commercial sportfishing boats that come down from San Felipe year after year, fishing the grouper every day from fall through winter and into spring. The spearfishermen must share the responsibility for their part in the taking of the grouper, but one commercial boat pulls out more grouper in a season than the entire tribe could in a lifetime. It is one thing to watch the abuse and disregard of an arid volcanic land, and it is another to see and feel the emptiness of a wilderness that a short time ago was overflowing with life.

I descend from the hill and the Christ figure, unaware of my future and blissfully immersed in the present, filled with the torrid energy of the Gulf. Frank intercepts me on my way back to camp and takes me to a shell beach which has been hidden from sight on the other side of the settlement. He speaks of a fine shell collection at home, a number of which were found on this very beach. Together we search the sand and find some dandies. Frank stares out into the Gulf and says, almost to himself, "Maybe next spring we'll try for Guardian Angel; you want to come along?"

5

WHITE SEA BASS

The white sea bass, yellowtail, tuna, bonito, barracuda, and other blue water pelagics are at the top of the oceanic food chain. They are intelligent and powerful, feeding at will on their inferiors. If they are healthy, they have no enemies other than man. Because of their intelligence and free reign in the ocean, they have a fearless curiosity which the spearfisherman tries to manipulate to draw the fish to within range of his speargun. There is no other way to do it. Chasing these fish is futile, tracking them impossible, and with the limitations placed on a breath hold dive, trickery remains the best method to get close. The yellowtail cannot resist an unaggressive intruder: it must see who or what is lying there motionless in the water. The bonito is similar to the yellowtail and may make a cursory pass before it moves on. Both species are much bolder when traveling in a school and will often circle a suspended diver

for his breath hold if his initial drop to depth is
not directly aimed toward the fish. The fickle barracuda must be approached with patience, the
diver never giving any hint of aggression. Generally, ocean predators can be temporarily tricked
in some way, and a thorough knowledge of each
species' particular traits will disclose their incli-
nations. The white sea bass is the exception: it
cannot be tricked. It must be stalked in the
untrackable waters outside the kelp beds.

The white sea bass is one of nature's most stun-
ning underwater creatures. Its color scheme begins with a fluorescent purple back that is mixed
with moss green at the edges. These colors gradu-
ate to silver just above the lateral line, and continue down to a belly that is snow white. As extraordinary as these colors are, when seen from
the surface they become absorbed in the lightless
fathoms, blending perfectly with the hue of the
depths, and rendering the fish almost invisible.
However, to see a white sea bass swimming at eye
level is to see a luminous ghost that has caught
all of the available light in the filtered depths and
reflected it back to the viewer. Unlike other free
swimming big fish, which are fueled by untiring
frenetic energy, the white sea bass moves with
effortless grace, and gives the illusion of gliding
through the water rather than swimming. The
very large ones appear to shoulder their way
along, their bodies swaggering under muscled
bulk. Like other creatures of exceptional beauty,
the white sea bass is cursed: its firm meat is delicious and is the best in these Pacific waters. The
unique behavior of the white sea bass lends credibility to its reputation for magical powers. A

member of the croaker family, it is the only deep water fish that emits a distinctive guttural sound. Many a hunter has chased its surreal croak until the sun went down, never seeing the fish. The white sea bass possess a sensitivity to the under-sea world that is indeed mysterious. It is an extremely shy and wary creature that upon sensing the slightest disturbance in the area, vanishes as quickly as vapor from a whale's blow. A fin splash on the surface, a slight noise from an anchored boat, a few bubbles escaping from a fin, even the infinitesimal sound of the human ear clearing through a pressure change can provoke flight. The white sea bass makes no grand exit in the tradition of its pelagic brothers; it simply disappears, nobody home.

The white sea bass is the most difficult of the Pacific pelagics to hunt. There are divers, good hunters, who have searched the ocean for over a decade looking for the fish and have never seen so much as a tail fin. Others have occasionally caught glimpses of their ghostly shapes as they evaporate into the depths. The white sea bass roam an inaccessible nether world of the ocean. For many, the only proof of its existence is when another hunter has landed one.

Those who hunt the white sea bass on a regular basis are a strange lot, a tribe within a tribe. They prefer to hunt the ocean alone, and go to great effort in discouraging others from entering their water. The lengths they go to see a white sea bass, much less to land one would be considered obsessive. They sacrifice warmth of head and feet by cutting holes in their hoods and booties so any air trapped in their suits can be released in the descent, and not escape during a crucial moment in the stalk. They have been known to grease their underarms and inside the legs of their wetsuits to avoid possible squeaks. They are in the water as the sun comes up and they are there after it has set. No sacrifice of inconvenience, cold or fatigue is too great. They are meticulous with their gear. Everything must be in perfect order before entering the water. Their spearguns are balanced pieces of work that are extensions of themselves, for there is no room for error when the fish are few, the opportunities fewer and the shot but one. They are engaged in a discipline that calls for patience, endurance, concentration and a wealth of knowledge.

To stalk the white sea bass successfully, the hunter must fill himself with the fish, knowing what it eats, when it feeds, and where its food source can be found. He must know the fish's patterns of travel in the morning, afternoon and evening, and be continually aware of changes in the environment—current, water temperature, visibility—and he must understand how these changes affect the movements of the fish.

There are several schools of thought in the approach to the actual stalking of the white sea bass. The first method, developed by the fathers when the fish were plentiful, was to dive an area selected through accumulated knowledge of the fish and the territory, and wait for the white sea bass to pass a particular point.

Over the years, as the white sea bass began to thin out, another method of stalking was developed by Al Schneppershoff. Al, a strong swimmer, chose to move continually, either on the surface

Charlie Sturgill with a sack full of abalone. Cica 1950.

Charles Sturgill (second from left) and friends. Circa mid-1940's.

Copper face mask that fitted above the nose, with equalizer air bulb attached, made in 1933 by Jack Prodanovitch. Copper goggles and camera housing were also constructed during that same period.

Jack Prodanovitch and Jim Stewarat with some fair-sized lobsters. Note Jack's eye glasses beneath his face mask. Photo by Lamar Boren.

Big Jim Christenson, before dry suits, wearing a wool sweater and wool pants (note short fins). Circa 1940's.

Jack and Wally with their ten-foot pole spears in 1944. Not a bad catch using arm-powered spears. Photo by Lamar Boren.

Jack with a 207-lb. broomtail grouper speared at Boomer Beach with power head pole spear in 1945. Photo by Lamar Boren.

Art Pinder (left) and Don Pinder (right) with a large Bahamian grouper. Taken with the small Hawaiian sling in Art's hand. Late 1040's.

Jack with his power head pole spear, and Wally with two grouper speared at Boomer Beach in 1946. Note the homemade face masks and cracked face plate and the ear plugs. Photo by Lamar Boren.

A day's catch—lobster diving in the early 1950's.

Art Pinder with his sail fish of 1948. How times have changed. (Note that Skin Diver Magazine *was for skin divers and spearfishermen.)*

Bill Hazen (left) and John Riffe with a white sea bass in 1949, using CO_2 spearguns, handmade snorkels and wearing the first commercially made face masks: Bill's from the Sea Net Co. (US), and John's the first one from France.

Jack Prodanovitch and Wally Potts returning from the La Jolla kelp beds on their paddle boards, with three big white sea bass. Early 1950's. Photo by Lamar Boren.

Fred and Art Pinder, the only spearfishermen ever to make the cover of Sports Illustrated.

Diver with his hands full. Photo by Omar Nielson.

Early 1960's in the Gulf. Diver bringing up a large grouper.

Coming out of the kelp with a yellowtail.

Jay Riffe and Lee Turcott with barracuda. Notice the half fish in Lee's right hand. Hammerhead was speared when it turned on the divers after it hit the fish.

Blue Water Meet 1971. From left to right: Tom Lolly, Carlos Eyles, Bob Sellers, Sid Campbell, Buzz Peterson, Bob Balleu, Al Schneppershoff, Mike Oceanus, Bob Stanberry, Will Brown. (Note the abundant white sea bass, shown on right side.)

Gulf Cabrilla. Photo by Omar Nielson.

Bob Stanberry with a 457-lb black sea bass. Photo by Bill Brown.

Hammerhead shark. Photo by George Kuznecovs.

Deep Pacific wahoo. Photo by George Kuznecovs.

Terry Maas and his blue fin tuna. Photo by Howard Benedict.

or under the water, seeking out the fish as one might seek out an elk in a forest. Al's success converted many of the second generation and today, his method is used by the majority of hunters. There are arguments for both methods; the way of the fathers permits longer bottom time because the hunter isn't moving and using up valuable energy. He is usually submerged and often in a good position for a decent shot. Al's method has the diver covering more area, and if he chooses his area well, he is likely to see more fish than the hunter who holds to a position. But if a fish is spotted from the surface, the stalker must be able to make his descent without being seen or heard; it is a moment of truth, and the hunter's technique must be impeccable if he is to have any chance at all.

The ocean conditions and the underwater topography usually dictate the method of the stalk, and the hunters often combine both methods if the area or situation calls for it. Regardless of which is used, the success rate, particularly in this last decade, is very low, so low in fact, that many of the old white sea bass hunters have given up altogether—too many weekends adding up to too many years with nothing to show for the effort.

Thirteen years ago this June, after hunting the fish for two seasons, I landed my first white sea bass off of Ship rock. In the water only minutes at the crack of dawn, I saw a flash below and dropped down to investigate. There in forty-five feet of water lay a school of white sea bass. My eyes devoured the sight: forty-pound fish, five feet in length and a foot and a half high, stacked twenty feet deep and fifteen feet across, all glowing in the depths. Although I made a clumsy descent the large school did not bolt away and I glided down, singled out a fish and let go an arrow. It was well placed and as the fish broke away from the school, I hung in the water spellbound in a kind of wondrous disbelief. I can still see it unfold with the clarity of this morning's sunrise.

The next ten years I lived for the summers and the white sea bass. I bought an old gas-hungry power boat and each weekend from May to the end of July, pounded over to the island and worked every kelp bed and pinnacle from the east end to the west end of Catalina.

My stalking techniques steadily improved until they were an unthinking response to both the fish and the environment. Hunting the white sea bass became second nature. I knew the fish as well as I knew myself. I had become a certifiable member of that eccentric group whose lives revolved around one fish.

"A hunter of shadows, himself a shade." Those who have hunted the white sea bass regularly over a long period of time often become connected to it in mysterious ways, and frequently find themselves directed to the fish by a source within them they cannot name. One of the earliest white sea bass hunters, Paul Hoss, tries to explain: "I can feel the fish when they are around; I positively know it, but I've never figured out how I know it."

Big Jim Christenson, who has probably landed more whites than anyone, says, "I can hear their tails moving." This from a man who, by his own admission, is deaf in one ear and hard of hearing in the other. But I do not doubt for a moment that Jim in some way knows when the fish are about.

"I've been in open water unable to see thirty feet beneath me in a hundred and twenty-foot bottom, feel the fish and drop down blind to sixty feet, and there will be a white sea bass. It has happened too often to be called coincidence."

There is little doubt that over a period of years a hunter can develop an affinity for white sea bass. On occasion I've found myself resting on the surface, empty, recapturing my breath, when all of a sudden it was time to dive. Following the call, I'd dive and see a fish either coming into view or just passing my position. Initially I believed it was luck. Later I realized that there might be some other influence coming into play. Yet it was not something I could make happen. Quite the reverse, usually it occurred when I was vacant and caught in the flow of the ocean.

***

The evening hour approaches, and after rechecking my gear for the third time, I dress to go. Putting my mask, fins, weight belt and speargun in the *Low Now*, I head out, running with a wind-chopped following sea that is coming from the northwest.

In ten minutes Eagle reef comes into view, and the thick matted kelp resting on the surface indicates zero current. A patch of sand glows green on the fifty-foot bottom. Quietly lowering the anchor, I follow it five minutes later, moving from one universe to another in an instant. The visibility is hazier than it appeared from the boat and it is difficult to make out detail past twenty-five feet, adequate for hunting, but far from ideal. This reef is several hundred yards long, running east to west, and broken into two sections. There are two high pinnacles on the western section that come within a few feet of the surface at low tide. From those high points the reef drops down to a fifty-foot bottom, then gradually descends to sixty, then seventy feet. The white sea bass like to breeze along the outside fringes of kelp surrounding the reef, seeking the bait that schools intermittently down its full length.

My plan is to swim down the reef on the south side and return on the north side, seeing how it sets up, finding where the bait lies and if there are any signs of predator feeding.

A school of anchovy sits on a single kelp stalk on the outside. Inspecting the school for chew marks and finding none, I move on down the reef examining other schools and watching hefty calicos scurry off into deep water. In fifteen minutes I reach the far end of the reef. There is a current beginning to build and at its head is a dense school of Spanish mackerel. Floating above the school, I watch it undulate like ripples on an ebony lake. Gradually the lake begins to split and a new river of fish branches off the main body like a tributary. A new leader has taken his constituents onto untresspassed territory. Then another break occurs and another river of fish forms; both still connect to the main body, each flowing as a stream, a river of fish within a current. The mackerel reconnect farther down and form a new lake. Swinging around the black lake of mackerel, I come to the north side of the reef and swim with the current. This side is absolutely barren; there is no bait, no calicos, not even an opaleye. Picking up my kick, I swim for the northwest end without making another dive. Reaching the west end of the reef, more Spanish mackerel congregate thirty feet down, and a large school of anchovies hovers ten feet above them. I drift over the school, waiting to see if flashes of its reflected light will bring predators. After ten minutes several large Pacific barracuda move on to the periphery of the anchovies. Dropping down on the skittish barracuda spooks them and they disappear into the blue haze, then cautiously return, watching me, watching the bait.

The barracuda move into the bait again and I descend, slowly facing away from their approach, and glide to their depth. Turning cautiously, I catch a look. At the movement of my head they drift away, but not out of sight. We play the game for twenty minutes, each dive brings me a foot or two closer until I can touch the fish with the fifteen-foot reach of the speargun. Twice I manage to maneuver close enough to pull off an imaginary shot, the last pull signaling the end of the lesson. There has been no encouraging sign beyond the barracuda, and somehow I don't believe that the white sea bass will be coming through here. Climbing back into the *Low Now* I motor toward the island and Two Goats.

The kelp is up and the water has the same haze that permeated Eagle, with perhaps an additional five feet of clarity. Cloud cover has darkened the sky and the bait fish reflect the mood, behaving as though feeding time were upon them. The fish on the perimeter of the kelp bed are nervous, moving in and out, inspecting me, then quickly departing. A minute and a half up, and a minute and a half down. This bed is an easy read for me. If there are fish in the area, they will have to come by this point of kelp. They have in the past. I dive the point for twenty minutes and see nothing. I'm resting on the surface and about to dive again when three small whites, each about ten pounds, cruise by close to the bottom, going with the current and in the opposite direction to my expectations. Diving at a slight angle to them, I close to within twenty-five feet without being seen. Suddenly they spurt off into deeper water, an unusual reaction for white sea bass. As the thought filters in, movement fills my peripheral vision, immediately I start for the surface and turn my head in the direction of the movement. Bearing down on me not thirty feet away are a mature gray whale and calf moving at a crisp pace. Taken completely by surprise, I push hard for the surface. The whales are equally startled and barrel just a few feet under my fins, bowling me into a backwards somersault from the concussion of their accelerated fluke action. The force throws my mask askew and it fills with water. I return to the surface with the clear message, "Stay alert; you're back in blue water."

On the next dive everything is as it was, the anchovies are huddled on the outside and the three-inch-long blacksmiths with their speckled blue backs hang motionless around a lone kelp stalk as I assume a position behind the same stalk. The ocean is still, yet tense. Down again, up again, watching, empty, dancing the dance. Down again and a bat ray sails by, the counterpart to the albatross of the skies. The bat ray with the smile of Buddha shows me the way.

I am convinced that there are pathways under the ocean; roads on which the pelagic fish and others travel. These paths fluctuate from day to day, probably from hour to hour, depending on the ocean conditions: water temperature, current, and who knows what other influences. I never really know where these paths will turn up on a given day, but it was the bat ray which first brought them to my attention. After watching these rays for years, I noticed that the white sea bass would often be moving at the same depth and in the same direction as a bat ray I had seen a short time before. Over a period of years this observation has been borne out eight times out of ten, and I've since adjusted my dives to the flight pattern of the bat ray.

A minute-and-a-half up and a minute-and-a-half down. The sun has dropped into the water and the early evening brings on a chill. After three hours in the water, I start talking myself out of the cold and fatigue. "I've only got a few dives left, this is the last one, just one more." But I keep making the dives, waiting and watching, looking left, then right. Keep the head moving, stay alert. Down again and there, coming through the outside fringe, shouldering its way around the stalks of the outside kelp at the same level as the bat ray, is a white sea bass. My position is good and in the dark water, the fish sees me too late and begins to veer away when it is almost directly in front of me. My arrow travels a scant ten feet before striking the fish several inches behind the gill plate. The white powers off into the darkening water with a burst of speed and is out of sight in an instant. The line zips through my gloved hand

and I tighten it, putting drag on the fish which briefly pulls me through the water. In ten seconds the fish stops running. It is in open water, and I follow the line out until it is perpendicular to the surface, then tie it off to the floating speargun. After relaxing for a few minutes, I dive to check the placement of the arrow and the condition of the fish. The white is holding position close to the fifty-foot bottom and the tip of the arrow has toggled, firmly securing the fish. I grip the arrow, and the fish stirs when I pull it toward me, sliding my hand up its belly into its gills.

Like the yellowtail of a week ago, the stalk unfolded with unexpected smoothness and I give thanks to the white sea bass for the generous gift of its life.

I fillet the fish by the light of the cabin lamp, eating pieces of raw flesh as I work. This little ritual began years ago. I liked the clean taste of the fish and the act just felt appropriate after a successful hunt. Many of the hunting tribes of North America believed that to eat the raw flesh of a highly respected animal would impart its special power and spirit to the hunter who brought it down. In addition to the North American tribes, African tribes and the Eskimos of the Arctic also ate the flesh of a freshly killed animal during the ceremony in their celebration of the hunt, thus sustaining strong connections with the natural world of which they were a part.

Working carefully on the fish, I make clean precise cuts, not wanting to leave any waste on the carcass. When the fillets are cut and removed, the tenderest morsels are cut out of the neck and belly. These are eaten and the carcass is consigned to the depths.

I find there is a distinct difference between the flesh of a wild animal and that of a domestic one. Wild animals seem to have a quality that is missing in domestic creatures. When we think of the conditions under which a chicken, for example, must live and grow then these differences become apparent. Chickens live in a dirty, crowded environment; they are fed processed foods filled with chemicals, they are filthy and weak. I think this kind of existence is bound to affect every fiber of that chicken's being; it is spiritless and incomplete. The white sea bass is as wild as an animal can be; free and mobile, it roams the underwater wilderness at will. It is alive because it is strong and must hunt for its food, eating other equally strong and wild creatures. The white sea bass is a clean, powerful and spirit-filled warrior living a life it was meant to live. This kind of existence must also affect every fiber of its being.

I question why I should accept a life that is any less noble than that of a white sea bass. But I have, and I do. Here on the *Infinity*, under these present circumstances, the way of the white sea bass becomes possible; here the ocean warrior can re-emerge, and I, at least for a time, can experience my life as I believe it was meant to be lived.

The following morning I grill half of the fish on a double hibachi rigged to handle the large fillets and nibble away on the cooked edges until I am filled. There is enough left for four or five future meals. I trade the other half away as I did the yellowtail a week ago. The locals highly prize the white sea bass and I receive a loaf of bread, some Italian squash, a handful of carrots, a head of let-

tuce, two tomatoes, a grapefruit, and a bag of potatoes in the barter.

The rest of the week is spent working on the
Infinity and catching up on my notes. In the eve-
nings, water conditions permitting, I explore new
areas within swimming distance from the boat.
The long kelp bed to the west looks promising for
game fish, but after a week of casual diving, I've
seen no fish moving through. These afternoon
dives have been lacking my normal concentration
and are more an attempt to stay fit for the annual
Blue Water Meet which is to be held here at the
island in seven days.

6

THE
BLUE WATER MEET

The Long Beach Neptunes' Blue Water Meet is billed as "The best spearfishing meet in the world, with the best spearfishermen in the world." There was a time when that declaration was very near the truth. These days I'm not so sure. But enough hunters still gather here for the meet to justify the billing, and it is more a gathering than a competition; the fathers are usually in attendance as well as the competition divers, and so of course are the blue water hunters.

The Blue Water Meet is unique, and differs from the standard spearfishing meet in every way. The typical competition, whether it is held in the United States or in Europe, is based on a point system; one point per pound and one point per fish, largest number of accumulated points wins. The Neptunes' Blue Water Meet, held at Catalina once a year, is invitational, and only game fish are eligible: white sea bass, yellowtail, barracuda, bo-

nito, tuna, and halibut. Only one fish can be sub-
mitted per diver; biggest fish wins. I like these
rules for several reasons. One, because along with
the necessary skill required to land a fish, luck
can also come into play, a factor which somewhat
equalizes the competition and gives each partici-
pant a chance, and two, only one fish may be sub-
mitted per diver. The latter is principally the reason why I participate and indeed is the very
element which separates the Blue Water Meet
from all other spearfishing meets.

The standard spearfishing meet has little appeal for me. I've entered only two, and that was
decades ago when I first became serious about
spearfishing. I admit that during the heat of the
competition the spearing of any decent-sized fish
that crossed my path didn't bother me all that
much. But it was afterward, when the multitudes
of dead fish were weighed, counted and measured
against those of the other competitors that it lost
whatever meaning I had given it. After my second
meet I permanently withdrew from the competitions. The rules levied in the Blue Water Meet
place a premium on the size of a certain species
of fish. And that, for me, makes the Blue Water
Meet worthy of its billing as "the best spearfishing
meet in the world."

My first invitation to the Blue Water Meet came
in 1971, several years before the fish population
began to drastically thin out. With four other
divers, I boarded a boat for a 3 AM crossing timed
so we could be in the water at first light. Big white
sea bass were running in thick schools then, and
five minutes out of the boat I came across a monster. I took what I thought was a good shot, but

the fish stripped a hundred feet of line off my reel in a matter of seconds, then wrapped around a kelp stalk and tore the spear free. Near the close of the meet, a lone yellowtail appeared just outside the kelp bed I was working and I was able to spear it and place fifth. The weigh-in is always held at noon. That day it seemed to me that all the greats of blue water were there: the best of the second generation and legendary fathers. Moving from one cluster of hunters to another, I drank in every moment, every word. At one point as I was describing the loss of the big white to another diver, Big Jim Christenson stepped up and joined the conversation. Speaking to me as an equal, he explained that there are two levels of blue water hunting, one with fish forty pounds and under and the other with fish over fifty pounds. He described the handling and rigging that a larger fish requires, and as he finished, the charismatic father from Italy, Gustav Della Valle, joined the circle of divers listening to Big Jim. Gustav went on about a grouper he had been stalking every day for two weeks somewhere in the Caribbean. He said the grouper knew what he was up to and by the end of the first week, waited for him each day thereafter to renew the chase. Into the second week the stalk continued, but Gustav could never get quite close enough. He said he had lost interest in spearing the fish. It was the pursuit, like that of women, that was so intriguing. The entire afternoon went that way; everyone on the beach lived and breathed the blue water and each had a hand in lifting it to the level that now existed. There was a strong sense of to-getherness among the divers and anyone in trunks was accepted as an equal member of the tribe.

The following year, ABC's Wide World of Sports sent a camera crew to cover the meet. It seemed doomed from the beginning. None of the hunters wanted a cameraman in the water because the noise would spook the white sea bass. ABC tried to cover Al, but they couldn't keep up with him in the water or in a boat. They chased him all over the island before giving up and trying another hunter, only to be met with the same problem. They didn't get any decent underwater footage that morning and managed only to record the weigh-in. Wide World of Sports never returned and blue water hunting was sentenced to the archives of video sport because it was labeled, accurately, a non-spectator activity.

In the eleven years I've participated, this will be my first opportunity to scout the island prior to the meet. I will use these next six days to scout the lee side of the island. Hopefully, I can locate an area that might consistently reveal an early morning congregation of white sea bass.

At 5:30 AM I rise from my bunk and look out the cabin door. Heavy gray skies fill my view and do not spark enthusiasm for jumping into a cold, damp wet suit. Still wrapped in a blanket I peer out of the starboard porthole for a better view: a foggy drizzle envelops the island. A warm invitation it is not. Forcing myself out of bed, I make tea, and breakfast on a sandwich, then sort my gear out on deck and climb into the dreaded wet suit which is indeed cold and damp.

The yellow skiff shoots west across a glassy sea that is now pockmarked by a steady drizzle of rain. The ocean is empty of other vessels and the rain adds a sense of removal from the outside world; it is at once lonely and peaceful. After a twenty-minute ride I reach the kelp bed called Starlight. It is one of the larger beds on the lee side of the island and historically has been a good morning spot for white sea bass.

There is a light current running so I kill the engine up current, drift down to the bed, anchoring on a sandy bottom in forty feet of water. I put on the rest of my gear and slip into the water. I am surrounded by a chilling stillness. As I pull the first rubber sling back into cocking position a whisper of reflected light catches my eye to the left, and there, fifty feet away, three white sea bass are moving across the bottom of a large kelp room; one fish is considerably larger than the others, perhaps forty pounds.

Quickly I cock the last two slings, then fall into silent running, moving to cut off the flight of the three fish. The current is with me and within a minute I reach the point where the fish should be coming through, but they are not there. Backtracking along their imagined course, I explore for alleyways within the deepening bed and find nothing. The whites have vanished.

The heavy stillness of the morning ocean is in sharp contrast with the electrical tension of the evening. The cold night lingers on the smaller fish and they make no attempt to escape when I pass. Even the flighty calicos are reluctant to budge from their position under the leaves of the larger kelp stalks when I come near. Swimming eastward against the current, I move to the end of the bed and the head of the current. In the twenty minutes it takes to reach my destination I've seen no fish, nor any point of kelp or school of bait that might draw them in. Arriving at the end of the bed, I find activity. Schools of anchovy drift halfway down to a forty-foot bottom and several medium sized barracuda are perusing the bait, making slow unaggressive passes, setting themselves up for a later feeding. This area looks good and I swim leisurely back and forth and up and down waiting for something big to blow through, but after a half hour nothing has come. I want to scout another bed while it is still early and before the white sea bass move out into deeper water, so I reluctantly leave this promising area and return to the *Low Now*.

Pulling anchor, I point the skiff west to a small bed which has no name, but has occasionally shown fish in the morning. It is a relatively small bed and easy to work. I settle into the water where a layer of surface haze obscures the bottom. I dive down and it opens up nicely to thirty-five feet. A school of anchovies drifts down a single kelp stalk that sits on the outside, away from the main bed. Moving above the anchovies, I let them be my eyes. Bait fish, particularly anchovies, have a marvelous system for staying alive in the ocean. They are willing to sacrifice a few to save many. The center of the school is dense and the fish fan out loosely from the main body. The fish on the periphery are the eyes for the rest of the school. Their movements alert the school when a potential threat nears it, and the fish bolt in the direction of the fleeing sentries in a choreographed race for survival. Waiting above the school, I watch it explode, then drop down toward the threat. It's a moment of uncertainty because I never know what has made the school jump until commitment to the dive is made. It could be a small calico practicing its hunting techniques, or a seal, or a shark.

I descend in time to see several bonito of medium size blaze by the anchovies at high speed, then veer quickly out of sight when I come into their view. Bonito are small pelagics that average four to six pounds in these waters, although larger ones to fifteen pounds will occasionally make an appearance. Their bullet-shaped bodies are silver with black horizontal stripes running the length of their backs, down to the lateral line at midbody. The bonito, with its arrow-headed, streamlined body and forked tail, is built for speed.

In the cloudy waters of the Pacific the fast moving yellowtail, tuna and bonito appear to materialize out of nowhere. One moment there is nothing but frosty blue, the next there is a fish ten feet ahead. If I'm looking in the wrong direction or my mind wanders momentarily, I will miss the fish or see it too late. These bonito have the speed and maneuverability of the swallows that dart so swiftly along the cliffs of Doctors Cove, and the eye can only track them for a few seconds before they disappear behind an aquamarine wall.

Twice more in the next twenty minutes, bonito swim into the school and veer off when I approach. This does not go unnoticed by the bait, and they move closer to me for protection and together we form a casual symbiotic relationship. But I cannot hold up my end; the point guards jump in warning and the flashing bonito hit the bait like lightning. So fast do they move that my eyes cannot follow the assault, only as the bonito move off at high speed do I catch a glint of a single sliver of light twitching between pointed jaws.

The bonito hold me to the school for another half hour, like the opening number for a big billed act, but the headliner never shows. I have been in the water for three hours and am shivering with cold beneath the wet suit. The sun has not breached the overcast sky and by the look of it, may stay hidden until mid-July. I decide to pack it in for the day and return to the *Infinity* for warmth, dry clothes and a nap.

The following morning the gray skies have re-fused to break and I see no encouraging sign that will lift me from the warmth of my bunk. There was a time, not that long ago, when I thought noth-ing of waking at two in the morning so that I could be in the water as the sun came up. Was it the abundance of fish which kept the chill factor in-consequential, or merely the burning desire that is youth's which insulated me from the cold morn-ings? Whatever the reason, it is gone now. Thoughts of the Blue Water Meet eventually pull me from my cocoon. In thirty minutes I've eaten, checked the gear and loaded it into the *Low Now*.

The water is the same glassy calm as yesterday and the *Low Now* slides east to Eagle reef, glid-ing on a mercury sea. The kelp is up, an encourag-ing sign, but when I get into the water the visibil-ity is no more than a disappointing eighteen feet, which makes surface scouting impossible. I'll have to drop down to around twenty feet and cruise at that depth along the outside border of the string kelp in an attempt to get as full a view as the vis-ibility permits. Moving down the outside of the reef, a current develops, pushing me lightly along just beneath the kelp where it bends. The black-smiths, señoritas, garibaldies and small calicos hang under the bow of the kelp trees, enjoying their solitude for perhaps the only time during the daylight hours. I reach the end of the reef in fifteen minutes, and as I suspected there is no activity here; it is up at the other end at the threshold of the rising current. Forced to swim against the current, I need thirty minutes of strong kicking and infrequent diving to make my way back to the west end. Reaching it, I find no fish or bait of any kind. This usually prolific reef is as still as a graveyard.

Back in the *Low Now* I scoot over to Ship rock. Here the kelp is bent to the same rising current, and that, combined with the lack of fish activity in recent years, is enough to discourage a jump. I decide to pass it up and go over to Isthmus reef.

Isthmus reef is the largest of the kelp beds on this side of the island. It would take several hours to swim around its circumference. Taking into account the current and previous knowledge of the area, I anchor in a section where I have found fish in the past. The current has become a force in the last half hour, so I'll swim into it for as long as possible, then when I tire, turn and use it to coast back to the *Low Now*.

The stillness of the undersea morning has fled somewhere between Eagle reef and here. This area is alive with fish activity; large calicos shoot for safety when I near; schools of bait hover in silver puddles close to the surface—there is tension in the water. Dropping down and latching on to a kelp stalk to hold my position against the current, I look out into the deep fringe for a breathhold, then let go and drift up again, move on the surface, then down again, holding on to the kelp, then up again, working my way west. Up and down, up and down, the current continues to build and the kelp that normally spreads out across the surface has stretched its full length several feet beneath the ceiling. Plunging into this rushing river under the sea has become work and in thirty minutes my legs, hot and tight, are beginning to tire. There is nothing left to do but turn and set sail with the current, which is now running at least four knots. Letting go, I soar along the tops of the flattened trees and reach the *Low Now* within minutes. Not a fish has crossed my path today and with the current as it is, no further diving can be done. It is ten o'clock in the morning.

For the next two days the pattern is the same: up early in the morning, check out new beds, re-scout Starlight, Eagle and No Name, all with the same results: no sightings.

While diving Eagle a boat comes quite close. Unable to determine how close it is to me (which is not unusual—all boats sound closer underwater than they actually are), I stay down and wait. Fifteen seconds later, the boat passes directly over me. This is not an uncommon occurrence for divers hunting in deep water; several have been hit and all have had near misses. There was a wrinkle in this one; when I surface and watch the stern of the boat pulling away, a trolling jig zips by my neck missing me by no more than a foot.

The current continues to rise, coming up earlier each day. By the time the meet is held on Saturday, it will be running by eight o'clock in the morning. The first few hours will be critical and probably determine the winner. After four days of scouting I've no more of an idea where the fish might be than I did the first of the week.

Friday afternoon I welcome my first visitor on board the *Infinity*, Monica, who joins me for the weekend to share in the festivities. She brings a large package filled with fruits, vegetables, nut bread and other assorted staples and my vow to live entirely off of the ocean is temporarily laid aside. We eat an early dinner and prepare to rise at 4:30 tomorrow morning. I want to be in the water at first light.

At 4:15 the stars still sparkle in the clear black sky; this will be the first sunny morning since I arrived twenty-four days ago. Monica awakens at 4:30 and is filled with nervous anticipation. We eat a light breakfast and drink some tea. Although the current will be a factor and probably restrict my hours in the water, Monica makes sandwiches anyway and I prepare myself for a five-hour dive. The black sky is giving way to navy blue as we load the *Low Now* with dive gear and prepare to shove off. Monica insists that she brings good luck to those who participate in events of this kind, offering references.

We head in the general direction of Eagle reef; nearing it, we see four boats already at anchor with divers waiting for enough light to make their jumps. Other boats filled with wet suited hunters buzz up and down the island heading for the spots they feel will yield the one big fish. On impulse I swing over to Two Goats. It is normally an evening spot, but less known than others and alone I stand a better chance of seeing a fish. Coming into Two Goats, I see another boat anchored on the east

side of the cove, so we motor to the west side and
anchor. Inexplicably the other boat pulls out. On
the alert for a good sign, I read this as one.

The sun is fifteen minutes away from the horizon when I disappear into the water, swimming
along the kelp line of the cove and out onto the
far edge of the bed. The water is dark and it is
difficult to see more than eight or nine feet. My
eyes strain for every inch of visibility. The current is asleep and the kelp is straight up. There
are few signs of life, everything is still or moving
in slow motion. I dive on an outside kelp stalk
that sits removed from the farthest point of the
main bed. The resident school of Spanish mackerel are lying low, barely moving in the chilly
dawn. I work up and down the pressure ladder in
an unhurried pace, finding my rhythm.

A large barracuda moves into the Spanish mackerel and stirs them out of their lethargy, I descend
on it in a dress rehearsal for white sea bass. The
barracuda doesn't see me until I have already
lined up the shot and pulled an imaginary trigger. Down and up, up and down, concentrating on
position, guessing where the paths might be from
the depth and direction where the barracuda
moved in on the bait. My bottom time is good: a
minute and a half down. In the water twenty minutes and no sightings, then thirty minutes, all
quiet. There are no boats or other divers in the
area, up and down, waiting, watching, out of
breath, come up slow, to my right, movement, a
white sea bass slightly above and behind me; the
fish has swum behind me on the inside! The white
is twenty-five feet away and the movement of my
ascent was slow enough not to spook it into flight,

but I have caught its attention. When I turn to line up with the fish, it moves further away. By the time I'm in position, it has gained an additional ten feet and is moving to depth. Several kicks push me closer, but the white is fully aware of me and continues to head for deep water. So far the fish and I have moved in slow motion, but if I am to get a good shot, I'll have to close the distance quickly and I'm afraid the movement will spook it and there will be no shot at all. As it is I am left with a long one that, under normal circumstances, I would rarely take. Three hard kicks close me to twenty feet. The fish, as though reading my mind, breaks out of its glide and starts to accelerate into the haze. When it does I let the arrow fly the full twenty feet. It strikes the fish and line jumps off the reel. A bad shot, the fish is moving at full strength. The arrow must have dropped in the distance it traveled and I've gut shot it. Just barely holding the line between my thumb and forefinger I let the fish take all it wants, thankful that it didn't swim into the kelp bed and wrap up. If it had, it would surely have broken loose from the arrow. Now it is out in deep water and I follow the line out to where it disappears into the depths. Gathering up the slack line, I tie it off to the floating speargun, then dive, tracking it down to fifty-five feet, where the fish is holding position just off the bottom. The arrow is dangling beneath it and the tip is visible, having caught a piece of skin just above the anus. I don't know what keeps the tip from falling out. I realize I can put no pressure on the line without risking the fish. Returning to the surface I know my only choice is to dive down without the white seeing me or hearing me, then grab the arrow and pull it to me and in the same motion slip my other hand into its gills. If I miss, or the arrow falls out, or the fish surges at the wrong time, it will probably break free. Relaxing on the surface, then hyperventilating deeply, I take one last breath and dive directly down on the fish. It is unaware of me until I reach for the arrow and accidentally brush against it. Startled, the fish lurches forward and I grab the arrow to pull it toward me, hoping the tip will hold. In the same motion I try to slip my hand into the gills, but they are closed. The fish is half loose and half caught and for an immeasurably long moment we struggle in the void. Finally the gills open up enough for me to slip my hand in and get a firm grip, then I kick my way to the surface.

Monica is sitting on the other side of the *Low Now,* gazing into the water and does not see me approach. When I heave the fish into the boat she yelps in glee and as she does the tip of the arrow falls from the fish and settles into the bottom of the boat. Exhausted from the long dive I lie across the seat in the middle of the *Low Now*. After a ten minute rest I return to the water for no other reason but to get back in for awhile. After forty minutes a current is beginning to build, so I head back to the skiff and suggest to Monica that we may as well go back to the *Infinity*. There we prepare a full sized breakfast and dine on the aft deck allowing the sunshine and our good fortune to sink in. When it is 10:30 we climb back into the skiff and head east to Rippers cove for the weigh-in.

Arriving just before 11:30, we find half a dozen boats already anchored and several people on shore digging out a pit barbecue. By noon, over twenty boats are drifting about the cove, looking for a spot to anchor. Several of these craft are commercial dive boats which have a broad beam and ample deck space for abalone and urchin as well as easy access to and from the water. They are built up in northern waters and Monica sees a similarity between these boats and chariots of Biblical times, the men standing with their black wet suits on riding at full speed across the water toward the cove.

Out of the sixty-seven divers who have competed, five have taken fish, quite a contrast from my first Blue Water Meet, when fourteen fish were taken by half as many hunters. A competition diver from central California wins the meet with a forty-three-pound yellowtail, a fine fish, which will be the largest yellow taken this season. A twenty-nine-pound white sea bass takes second and my twenty-seven pounder, third.

The pit barbecue is going, the beer is being drunk at a steady clip and the stories are already in high gear. I wander through feeling as if I have been resurrected from the dead, but as the gathering breaks into groups, I notice only a few of my old chums from the second generation: Bob Donnell, Yas Ikeda, Dale Coty, Bob Ballew and several others. Only two fathers are in attendance, Charlie Sturgill and Dick Jappe. All the others are acquaintances or strangers.

"Where is Bob Stanbery?" I ask Dale.

"Ear problem," he replies.

"Where are the others?" I ask Bob Donnell, who more or less organizes this affair.

"I thought more would come, but they didn't

show. I don't know where they are; fewer from our generation come each year. Where have you been?"

"There are a lot of new faces here," I say.

"Big game spearfishing is becoming popular," Bob replies. "There are more people participating now than ever before."

"How can they develop the skills with so few fish?" I ask. "Do they go to the Gulf or some other remote spot where there are still big fish?"

I am told of one newcomer who wishes to buy a world record fish by going to a faraway place and spearing a species that few can reach.

Someone says, "If he wants to be a true hunter of fish, let him bring in a white sea bass. He doesn't have to travel the world to prove anything to me."

"Hell, there ain't no fish anymore," says Charlie. "You can bust your ass out there for days, weeks even, and see nothing. Seventy percent of the game fish are gone and ninety percent of the abs are gone. It's no fun—a lot of work for nothin'."

"I've seen white sea bass; they're still out there."

"Not that many," says Dick Jappe. "What chance do you think these kids have of seeing one? I'll tell you: almost none—never mind spearing one."

Charlie: "Maybe yellowtail. If the yellows keep comin' in, they could learn on the yellows. It comes and goes; you never know when the fish will be in from one year to the next."

Dick: "It's not like the old days when there was fish taken on practically every trip. We didn't have the equipment then. Now they got the best equipment that can be made and there's no game fish."

"What about the Gulf?" I ask.

Bob: "Sure, there are spots left in the Gulf, but no one gives away secrets anymore. If you got a spot or two in Baja, you keep it to yourself and go with a partner who is not about to tell anyone. Do you think anyone is going to tell these guys where the fish are?"

Charlie: "To hunt big fish any more you got to have time and money, and plenty of both. Blue water hunting is turning into a rich man's pastime."

"Yeh, but those who can learn with the thinning fish population ought to be pretty good hunters," I say.

"That might be true," says Dick, "but they'll never be as good as the hunters of ten years ago, and there will never be another better than Art Finder; he was the best that ever lived."

An unusual statement for a California diver about a Florida diver. It has credibility, coming from Dick Jappe, who has seen them all, and has competed longer than anyone in the history of the sport, including Art.

Dick continues, "I saw Art do things in the water no man could ever duplicate, especially down in his part of the country. I remember when we were down in Florida, scouting for the Nationals and Bobby Weaver was coming up from a long dive with a bleeding fish. And here comes this shark barreling up from the bottom heading straight for Bobby. We were five of the best spearfishermen in the country, and all we could do was watch from the surface. Bobby was too deep, and it was happening too fast. But Art, he drops down with that Hawaiian sling of his and somehow, I still don't know how, gets close enough to throw an arrow into the shark's nose when it is only a foot away from Bobby's leg. Art was head and shoulders above the rest of us when it came to hunting too. I've just never seen better in the fifty years I've been diving."

Soon the beer is gone and the food has been eaten. The stories have given way to cleaning up and the party dissolves. There is a channel to cross and a home for the divers to return to. It all breaks up quickly, and we're back in the *Low Now,* pushing our way west to the *Infinity*.

The glow of the day keeps us up until well after midnight. There was magic in this day and I refuse to yield to sleep, knowing how few of these moments there are in a lifetime.

7

WILD CURRENTS AND OTHER MOVING EXPERIENCES

When scouting for the meet two weeks ago, I thought the underwater terrain at No Name looked ideal for hunting white sea bass in the evening. The water conditions have been poor due to the relentless currents and I've been waiting for the water to clear so that I can test my hunch. These last days the current has begun to ease up around sundown, an encouraging change that begs for an early evening dive.

A late afternoon breeze has built a moderate sea that the skiff pounds into for forty minutes before reaching the bed. Entering the water, I find a mild current running, but the visibility is a surprisingly clear thirty to thirty-five feet, enough clarity to make out a white sea bass from the surface. Moving to an outside point of kelp, pumping up and dropping down, I suspend at twenty-two feet and clear my suit of air. The ocean feels like home now; the uneasiness I felt a month ago has steadily fallen away and I am once again the light, free swimming hunter. Kicking easily against the current to hold position, I watch the outside fringe, expecting the fish to be swimming up into the current. Up again, down again, for half an hour I dive the area. My dives are rhythmical and fluid. I move with confidence to depth and back again, without thinking about the length of my breath hold or the depth of the dive. No longer encumbered with self doubts or my mainland past or future plans, my head is empty of every thought except what is here before me, under the water.

The Spanish mackerel that were here two weeks ago have fled, leaving the blacksmiths fastened in position on the outside fringe like specks in a blue ice cube. Up and down, watching the outside line of kelp. While waiting back on top, resting, I see twenty-five feet down cruising along the outside line and materializing out of the haze a white sea bass. Using a kelp stalk for cover, I drop down and level off at the same depth as the fish. It's moving slowly east. Swimming to it, I keep a line of kelp between us. The white sea bass follows the kelp line as it cuts in toward the island and me. Intercepting the fish when it is fifteen feet away, I close to ten feet and let the arrow go. It hits the fish just above the lateral line, striking the backbone and killing it instantly.

I couldn't have executed the stalk any better, nor had a cleaner kill. I knew the fish would be mine when I first saw it, as though the outcome had already been determined. Do other predators in nature have that moment, when they know before the prey is caught that it cannot escape? If their instincts are true, I imagine that they do know, and I would also imagine that the prey would never know.

The *Low Now* and I are running with the sea, skiing down the easterly moving swells, heading for the *Infinity*. The rolling sea penetrates the skiff and finds its way into my bones, and the powerful breath of nature blows into my face. The smells of the fish and sea become one, flowing through me unchecked by any idea that could separate me from any part of it; at this moment I have no doubt that here is where I belong.

Coming around a dogleg of the island, a red hulled boat shows its colors on Eagle reef. At this time of the evening I would guess it to be Bob Stanbery and Dale Coty. Reaching their boat, I find Dale and Jerry Brewer on board and Bob in the water. The conversation is terse. "Have you seen fish?"

"Yes, but current is tearing the water up real good."

Bob gets aboard his own boat. He sees the white and says, "Did you get it up at Starlight?"

I lie and say, "Yes." Bob looks at me with a half-smile. He knows I won't tell him where I got the fish, just as I know he wouldn't tell me. White sea bass hunters are a closemouthed bunch; they want no one else in their water. Secrets are only shared when you ride in the same boat. So there is little to talk about other than the water conditions, and the meeting is brief. They want to dive another spot while there is still light. We wish each other luck, and part.

Returning to the *Infinity* I see that another boat lies anchored off her starboard beam, a twenty-five-foot Coronado, the *Godwit*, skippered by

Roger and Sioux, whom I came to know as this journey of mine progressed into summer. I like the looks of them, he with a yellow beard and warm smile, and she with gorgeous brown hair falling down her backside. I offer them a cut from my fish after I have completed my filleting ritual. They accept the fish and in return Sioux gives me several meals' worth of dehydrated vegetables. They have worked out a fine system of existence without the need for refrigeration, using dehydrated vegetables, eggs, noodles, dried fruits, and assorted other goods as well as sea food when they can get it. Later in the summer they give me the details of their system and I show Roger how to hunt for food.

During the night the wind rises steadily, peaking at around midnight, and the *Infinity* strains against her anchor lines and pounds the water beneath her bow. Around 4 AM it dies enough for me to fall asleep. I wake at 8 AM, make tea and go topside to greet the new day, sipping tea on the *Infinity's* aft deck. On the nearest ridge directly astern of the boat, not seventy-five yards away, stands a lone male buffalo, grazing on the already yellow grass of the early California summer. It turns to my movement and we stand in our separate worlds, eyeing one another.

During the 30's a movie company imported the buffalo as background for a western film. Rather than transport the animals back to the mainland after the picture was completed, they stayed and were given sanctuary and free run of the island. I understand that this is only one of two wild herds of buffalo left in the country; certainly it is the only herd that can be seen from a boat. Over the last fifty years the buffalo have steadily multiplied and today, the herd is large enough to remind us of a past when wild creatures dominated the land and were intimately involved in the ebb and flow of the natural world.

The buffalo is a proud-looking beast with a large head and impressive horns. Scruffy and tough, it has the confident look of a wild animal, a formidable one that would call for skill and courage to bring down with arrow or lance. So rich was the buffalo's gift to the Plains Indians that it permeated their culture; they wore its skins, ate its meat, used its tendons for bindings and its bones for tools and in ceremony. The very survival of many of these tribes was dependent on the buffalo. So it was natural to assume that the beast was the supreme gift from the Great Spirit. Further, it also represented a direct channel back to the Great Spirit through which the tribe could communicate, offering, in ceremony, thanks for its gift.

Initially, the white sea bass appeared to me as though it were a gift from a higher entity, and if not a higher one, certainly a greater one—the most powerful on the planet, the ocean. However, as my hunting skills increased and I became proficient at stalking the fish I gradually abandoned this idea, believing instead that it was my hunting prowess alone that was putting fish in the boat. This attitude did not alter my productivity. I continued to bring fish in at the same rate, but after a while I felt less like a hunter and more like a killer. I was unmindfully taking from the ocean. And with that attitude there came an unsettling emptiness. So hollow did it leave me that after several seasons, I had to re-examine my mo-

tives for hunting; I had lost the wonder and joy of
it. When I finally realized that it was my narrow,
egocentric view of simply taking, rather than the
idea of the ocean providing, I returned to the water prepared to accept whatever gift the ocean
offered and be grateful for the opportunity. Thus
my responsibility as a hunter is to receive the gift
as impeccably as another ocean predator accepts
its food. It also follows that if I am not ready to
accept the gift, in all likelihood it will not be seen
or be seen too late, or an error in judgment will
keep it from my hand. The actual spearing of the
fish, although exciting, becomes no more important than stalking, or cleaning, or cooking, or eating, or the elimination of my waste back into the
sea. It all becomes a circle.

***

The current becomes a raging river for five
straight days and only lets up to change direction. It snatches up every loose speck of dirt, silt,
waste and debris and sweeps it down the island.
Yesterday the force of the current broke loose the
Infinity's stern anchor. It was strange to come up
on deck and see that the walls of my cove had
somehow been rearranged. The bow anchor was
holding firm; there was not much I could do but
wait until the current lifted enough for me to re-
anchor. It was an uneasy night; if the current
shifts, we're in the rocks on the port side. I stayed
topside through the night watching the current.
If it shifted, I would have started the engine and
either held position with the prop or pulled out
to sea. An hour before dawn the current subsided

and I swam out and re-anchored in a rock out-cropping near the beach.

Today the current has churned the water up so badly that it is impossible to see more than ten feet on the outside. The water inside the kelp beds close to the island is clearer, protected to a degree by the surrounding bed. I still have meat from the white sea bass speared six days ago, so my need to dive is not through my stomach. The urge arises from another source. Following my impulse, I swim out to a point of kelp east of the *Infinity* where I have noticed the best visibility over these last six weeks.

The water temperature has changed; the ocean is several degrees warmer. On land when the weather warms, eggs hatch, bulbs sprout and the ground becomes an incubator for everything that squirms, wiggles and crawls. The ocean is no different, except the life that springs forth is minuscule and the remnants of their births and bloomings hang in the atmosphere like opaque particles of dust. Trying to see in this water is like looking through a pane of sky blue frosted glass. If I were to spear a fish it would have to swim over, give me a nudge then back off a foot so that I might make out its shape in the thick mist. I dive deep, hoping that the visibility will open up farther down as it sometimes does, but without the reflected light the milkiness turns to brown haze and I'm suspended in a dusty 3x3x3-foot room. Fish suddenly appear, then just as quickly disappear. There is no real contact with anything; this world has no bottom, no depth of field, no definition, ghostly objects fade in and out of focus, as in a dream.

When I began to dive the blue water and the conditions were similar to what they are today, my imagination would take control and conjure up sharks lurking just beyond my range of visibility. The dirtier the water became the more my imagination would unleash its fear-filled drama. I very nearly drove myself out of the water. Now the water is no more than a foggy room that remains unchanged no matter where I choose to move. Despite the frustration of being unable to see, it does feel good to be in the water and I move up and down vigorously experimenting with the limitations of my vision, seeing if there is another way to see.

Another week and the current remains a wild and unchecked floodgate. My time is spent working on the boat, reading and writing. Usually I wake with the sun and drink several cups of tea while sitting aft, watching the morning light bring the island to life. The island birds greet each day with their song and the sea birds are already scouring the water for a meal. The pelicans are most evident, flying in formation, working the water like notes moving up and down the scale on an azure sheet of music. The edges of their wings, like fingers, caress the quarter inch of air just above the water, then rise to gain a higher note, building momentum until they can slide down the scale and begin their song again.

After tea I do some tai chi movements to loosen my body, then sit down to write. My first meal of the day is lunch and I'll eat some fruit and whatever can be made into a sandwich. After lunch and a short nap I usually spend several hours working on the boat. With the visibility as poor as its been, I may do some line fishing for dinner or skin it across the cove for an abalone. I discovered a small colony of green and pink abalone within swimming distance of the *Infinity*. I usually eat a seafood dinner of some kind, and wash it down with a glass of wine, then read or listen to music before going to bed an hour or so after sunset. This way of life agrees with me. I've lost weight, yet my strength and endurance have increased. When this journey began I wondered how I would cope with the loneliness and boredom, but I have experienced neither. The solitude is a luxury and this life is far from boring.

As I observe the daily comings and goings within the cove, it becomes evident that the creatures of the sky and sea spend as much time at play as they do at work, particularly the birds. The island swallows are forever involved in a game of tag, darting about the ridges of the island in flashy displays of speed and maneuverability. An inseparable pair of crows remains close to the cliffs, cavorting in the updrafts with the gulls and conversing on the ledges and in the hollows of those high walls. Lately I've been able to imitate a few of their sounds and we call to one another in a language only the crows understand. Occasionally a blue heron visits the cove and forages in the saltwater shallows at sundown; it stands as a lonely, solemn figure against the glow of twilight, a contrast to the active play surrounding it.

Last week a flock of pelicans discovered a thermocline a half mile east of the anchorage and caught it, spiraling upward thousands of feet until they reached a hidden air stream, then shooting northward with fixed wings on unseen rails until they were out of sight. And for what reason? Why do the dolphins converge on a passing boat, swimming and diving beneath its heaving bow for as long as the boat is moving in the same general direction as the school? Why do the seals go into their barrel rolls and loop de loops when I swim among them? Is it something more than play and the expression of joy for being alive? In contrast I see the heron in me, serious and occupied with daily patterns. Where is my own play? Over the years have I forgotten how to let go to the joy of living and express it in play? Not competitive or social play, but the abandoned play of the child and the dolphin. Watching nature from my vantage point, I see my need to frolic and express the joy for being alive.

Acting on the spur of the moment, I leap into my wet suit and jump over the side of the boat with no other motive but to have fun. Swimming to the kelp bed next to the cliffs, I dive into the hazy shallows and greet the first inhabitant that comes my way, a garibaldi, the bright orange fish of the perch family that is indigenous to these waters. The garibaldi are protected by California law and have apparently been so informed; they fearlessly flaunt their immunity. Because I am a visitor, I feel that it is only polite that I make a friendly gesture. Breaking open several sea urchins, I spread the exposed parts on the ocean floor so that they can dine on the roe. The noise of the breaking urchins reaches out into the water like a dinner gong and soon there are a dozen garibaldi dining freely on a delicacy for which the Japanese pay handsomely.

The garibaldi is an enigma; on one hand it can

lead a diver to hidden caves and holes he might never ordinarily find; its bright color makes for easy tracking around the stone labyrinth of a reef. On the other hand, once these occupied holes are discovered the garibaldi will actually block these entrances with its body, shielding the lobster inside and allowing them to retreat to safety. Here is a civilization of which we know very little, particularly in the relationships among the creatures.

Tracking one of the orange fish, I discover a large hole. Inside are several black abalone and two small lobsters that recede into the back of the cave when I appear in the entryway. Cautiously, they reappear and extend their feelers in greeting; we touch, finger to feeler, in a traditional gesture of friendship. They have little to say; frankly, I don't think they trust me.

Shifting my attention to the abalone, I carry the conversation. Knowing that their life is difficult and their numbers have been severely reduced in the last two decades, I ask about the hardships they must endure. They tell me of a time during the late eighteen hundreds when the sea otter still ranged down the western edge of the North American continent. The ravenous eating habits of those furry sea creatures decimated the abalone, and continually had them on the edge of extinction. Then man came along in his sailing ships at the turn of the century, seeking the coats of the sea otter, and in the space of ten years wiped the otter out. Without knowing it, man tipped the ecological scales in favor of the abalone and over the next forty years, they multiplied in such abundance that every available rock and reef was stacked with them. I had assumed the abalone were always plentiful until man had found his way into the ocean and begun to harvest their population. "Not so," said the abalone. "Man saved us from the otters, but now he has turned on us and we fear the same fate as the otter." There was not much I could say in the way of assurance. Man had, on occasion, corrected his mistakes; perhaps he would again. They shrugged their shells in the manner that abalone do. "Perhaps," they said, with little conviction.

Despite my awareness of the plight of the abalone, I am enjoying myself. With speargun or camera in hand, I tend to focus on the underwater world that holds my special interests. Unencumbered by those limitations, events seem to freely fall my way. One of the by-products of play is that it loosens up the structure of regular patterns and permits entry of new information that might never be considered valuable or important. "In seeking nothing, I behold everything."

Locating another cave, actually more a tunnel, I come eye to eye with a large calico, maybe ten pounds. We stare at one another for a moment, then the hunter in me wishes for a speargun. As instantly as the thought forms in my mind, the calico splits out of the rear entrance of his afternoon lodgings. In this telepathic environment one is responsible for one's thoughts. Pure in deed is not enough when attempting to make small talk with a calico.

I watch a medium-sized bat ray of fifty pounds fly over a large rock studded with brilliant yellow bulbs. The messenger with the perpetual smile whom the dictionary inaccurately labels devilfish.

Descending on the ray and intercepting its flight, I swing parallel to it and glide with it for a while. Finally, I ask the question that has been haunting me for years. Once, while hunting off of the east end of San Clemente Island, I witnessed one of those natural phenomena that every so often man is privileged to see: an armada of bat rays, in the thousands, swimming in a formation ten feet thick and thirty feet across. Wave after wave flew by. When I dove into their midst, they peeled away to avoid me and regained position after they passed. On they came; for twenty minutes they passed my position until the last had winged by and was gone.

"Where were they going?" I inquired. "Where had they assembled?"

The smiling bat ray said, "We each have our journey; sometimes we share it, sometimes we go alone." And with a sweep of its wings it disappeared into the haze.

***

Another week slides by and the current moves with a will of its own. When it does come to rest periodically during the day, there is not enough time for the underwater soot to settle before it begins again, and the blue water remains undiveable. I consider taking the *Low Now* on what would be a day's run to the windward side of the island. Usually the water is rougher on the backside because in addition to the current and wind, it takes the full brunt of the Pacific swells. When the conditions are good on the backside, the diving is excellent. Blue water hunting at Catalina really began here. In the late 50's and early 60's great schools of white sea bass and yellowtail moved through from Church rock to Silver Canyon. It was there in the Silver Canyon area that the giant black sea bass were discovered in large numbers. The black sea bass are different from the other Pacific game fish, because they tend to stay in one area rather than roam up and down the coast. In addition, they grow to an enormous size, over six hundred pounds.

The fathers had run across the black sea bass in their early travels, but their equipment was fragile and incapable of holding these powerful fish. Later, the second generation discovered the blacks in large numbers and aggressively hunted the fish throughout the sixties and seventies. Unfortunately, the black sea bass were often taken for trophy rather than for their edible qualities. Black sea bass are good eating up to several hundred pounds; beyond that their meat begins to get stringy and tough. Usually the divers turn the big ones over to orphanages, prisons or other charitable organizations whose customers' complaints would go unregistered.

The black sea bass is one of the more dangerous fish in the Pacific. Its strength and power are such that the hunter cannot control it once speared, and it usually takes several hours of hard diving to subdue it. The fish is particularly dangerous to the diver attempting to bring it to the surface. Loose floating line can loop around an arm or leg, or catch a weight on a weight belt, and in one of the many runs the fish makes, the diver can get caught and pulled down without any chance of stopping the fish. It has happened before: Morrie Rothstein drowned off Santa Cruz island in 1969 when the black he speared took him down.

The premier black sea bass hunters were of the second generation and there were several, with Bob Stanbery and Al Schneppershoff of Los Angeles and Paul and Joe Herrin of San Diego standing above the field. The four of them traded the black sea bass record around for years. They all had different styles of hunting the fish. The Herrins had exceptional bottom time, over two minutes a dive. They dove deep and fearlessly, and knew their territory well. Al could not cut the deep dive but covered the surface so quickly and mindfully that his well trained eye could spot the fish in the depths where others saw nothing. Bob was somewhere between. Yet they all had this uncanny sense for the fish. One might think it easy to see a four or five hundred-pound fish swimming around in the water. It isn't. Usually, movement catches the eye of the hunter. The blacks move very little and when they do move, it is usually slowly and close to the bottom. Their dark coloring blends into the depths, making them difficult to see even under the best conditions. On one of my rare black sea bass outings with Bob I asked him what his technique was for seeing the fish. He said he looked for holes or blank spaces in the ocean terrain and that would be a fish. His eye for the ocean topography was so complete he was able to see the subtle unfamiliarities within the familiar.

Hunting black sea bass is not my forte. I don't have the eyes or desire for them. My interest is in white sea bass. The day I did spear a black, I

was looking for whites off of Church rock on the
backside and only by chance did I happen to see
the big fish suspended near the sixty-foot bottom.
Improperly rigged for black sea bass, having no
cable, or poppers, (balloon-like self-inflatable CO_2
floats), I was nonetheless irresistibly drawn to the
fish. The black was larger than any fish I had seen
in the ocean. Diving directly down on it, I placed
an arrow into its shoulder then kicked for the
surface. By the time I reached the top, all one hundred and seventy feet of line on my reel was gone
and the black was dragging me steadily out into
the open ocean. After ten minutes and some distance from the island, unease crept into me; how
was I going to stop this fish? I had no help, and no
one knew of my situation.

I've been misplaced before in the open ocean
and know how easy it is to become a tiny dot lost
among the swells. Eventually, the situation
righted itself when after another ten minutes, the
fish abruptly turned and headed back to the island. When I was within swimming distance of the
anchored boat, I let loose my speargun and returned to the boat for another. It often takes two
or three arrows to subdue these huge fish and I
put another into it, but could not bring it down.
Kicking continuously, I would pull the fish up and
when it neared the top, it would turn and make a
run to the depths, the floating line whipping
straight as it followed the fish down. It went that
way for two hours until I was able to finally bring
it to the surface and put a stout line through its
gills. The black was too heavy for the three of us
to haul into the boat, so we lashed it to the swim
step for the channel crossing. It weighed two hun-

165

dred and seventy pounds and fish dinners were eaten for months among family and friends, until the invitations began to be politely refused and we had to finish it ourselves.

In a similar incident, Bob Stanbery was not so lucky. He and Al were diving for blacks at San Clemente island, which lies fifty miles off the coast, and Bob got into one that dragged him out to sea. His attempts to stop the fish were little more than applying as much drag on the fish as he could without being pulled under. When night finally fell, Bob was several miles out in open ocean. Al had no idea what had happened or where his partner could possibly be. Having no knife to cut the line and keep the speargun, Bob had to release it and try and make his way back to the island in the dark. Swimming for several hours through strong currents and heavy seas, he reached the inner waters of the island, where Al had been tracking back and forth in the night, searching for his companion. Bob was near collapse when Al found him and hauled him aboard. Every so often there is a report of a speargun being towed at a steady pace between the islands of Catalina and San Clemente. There is a belief that the day it is retrieved will mark the beginning of the last days for the blue water hunter.

Near the end of the 70's a moratorium was placed on the taking of black sea bass, and I was glad to see it. The skill and courage required to hunt these fish notwithstanding, the taking of a fish (or any animal) for any reason other than for food never set right with me. Today these mammoth fish can exist in peace, and, like the buffalo, stand as a reminder of a time when their great

numbers were a part of another grand order of
which we still know very little.

8

CUTTING THE
BLUE EDGE

The currents and poor visibility confine my
hunting to the inside kelp. Stalking these
beds is a rediscovered joy, and wholly different
from that first week when I labored through these
same beds. In the water and loose as a jellyfish, I
work the bed like a seal, picking out the fish that
fills my immediate needs.

Diving the kelp beds satisfies my desire to get
into the ocean, but my heart swims in blue water.
There is a purity to the deeper water that pulls
me to it the way a mountaineer is pulled to the
rarefied air of the mountain peaks, where man
leaves no trace of himself as he does in the foothills and in the kelp beds, where his discarded
junk remains an ugly signature in an otherwise
perfect kingdom. Out in the blue water as on the
high mountain ranges, no such evidence of man
(or very little of it) exists. And in that unpredict-
able country where life and death are always

present, there is generated in me a state of alertness that I cannot summon up on my own; out there in blue water I am the best that I can be.

At the end of the week the visibility begins to show signs of improvement. Brief excursions outside the kelp are encouraging. After three days of waiting for a definitive change, I decide to try a morning hunt before the ocean is stirred by the currents that rise with the winds in the afternoon.

The breaking sun inflames the island, turning it gold as the *Low Now* points toward Two Goats and makes good time over an ocean that is slick as ice. The floating kelp gives evidence of currentless water and the visibility from where I sit in the boat looks diveable. Quickly suiting up, I slide into the water where my enthusiasm instantly deflates; the water is milky, less than twenty feet of visibility. Without bothering to cock my speargun, I return to the skiff. Sitting in its stern, discouraged and frustrated, I look out absently over the water and my gaze falls on Ship rock. Ship rock is the deepest of all the dive sites on the lee side of the island and some of the largest fish ever taken have been found there; it was where I speared my first white. Over the years the sea lion colony that inhabits the fifty by seventy-foot rock have multiplied freely, and they have become a nuisance to the spearfisherman. Their hunting and cavorting about the rock spooks the fish which cruise the outside edge of the dropoff. The sea lions have turned this once great hunting area into a rookery, and the tribe has given up on it.

"I've tried everywhere else, why not the rock," I ask the *Low Now* as it surges forward to the

white, dung-covered pinnacle. Watching the anchor descend to the top of the plateau thirty feet
down revives my sagging enthusiasm. The water
is definitely clearer here. Upon entering the water, I find the visibility to be a sparkling fifty feet.
The rock is much like the tip of a mountain with
small plateaus jutting out of the east and west
faces. These plateaus are twenty to thirty feet
deep and extend away from the rock approximately a hundred feet then drop sharply down to
a bottom of a hundred and ten feet. The north and
south faces fall away at a sharp incline down to
the same twenty fathom bottom. This is blue water country and there is tension in the nervous
movements of the fish occupying the dense kelp
bed on the eastern slope where the *Low Now* is
anchored. Swimming through the kelp toward the
south drop, I see a school of large calico, all eight
to ten pounds, congregating around the base of a
deep kelp stalk. One eyes me and drifts off the
stalk, signaling to the others that the meeting is
over, and the gathering silently adjourns.

When I drop to thirty-five feet, patches of sand
become visible on the bottom eighty feet below.
Blacksmiths in the thousands stretch from the
surface to the depths and out to sea beyond my
vision. Moving to the southeast side of the rock
and making another dive to forty feet, I watch a
large male sheepshead with vivid black, red and
white markings graze on the rocks far below. My
bottom time is brief, and as I rise to the surface
two sea lions rush by me from behind, and in the
heavy stillness give me a jolt. They spin their way
down eyeing me with uncertainty.

Continued swimming around the circumference

of the rock, kelp points and outcroppings bring back memories of other days and other fish. Today only the southeast face shows signs of activity. Returning to the blacksmiths and dropping into their crowded midst, I inspect the small fish for signs of predator feeding. Several have been chewed on and the white rake marks indicate that the feeding was recent, within two days.

While lying on the surface trying to make something out of the marks, a faint movement draws my attention to the deep water below. Descending to forty feet, I see three white sea bass, all big, all over fifty pounds, swimming north to south in seventy five feet of water. I continue to drop, but the broad angle of my descent in the open water is easily seen by the whites and they turn off into the hundred-foot bottom and dissolve into it.

"So this is where they are," I tell myself, feeling like one who has just stumbled onto the lost and fabled elephant burial grounds, "feeding at their pleasure on blacksmiths." The sighting pushes the outside world into oblivion and the ocean itself evaporates; there is only the white sea bass, hidden somewhere in the deep water. I work the area for fifty minutes but the fish have not reappeared, and I've the distinct feeling that none will. My dives are not deep enough to properly pursue the fish anyway and this disadvantage further convinces me to retire for the day. A diving accident seven years ago severely damaged both of my ears and continued deep diving tends to fill the middle ear with fluid, so I'm reluctant to push for depth. I'll return early tomorrow morning when the fish are likely to come up higher to feed.

Seeing white sea bass that size is a rare and thrilling sight, and their images swim before me throughout the day. Because of the depth the fish are running, I decide to change spearguns and use the teak gun. It has a Mexican rigging, no reel, just the speargun with a hundred feet of polyethylene line attached to the shooting line and a small float secured on the other end. After a fish is speared, the line runs free from the speargun, allowing me to surface without being physically connected to the fish. Once on the surface I can grab the buoyed line and begin working the fish. This type of rigging works best in open water and away from kelp that could tangle the free-floating line as dives are made. After spending several hours preparing the speargun, selecting the proper arrow and setting up the rigging, I'm confident that everything is in perfect working order.

The fish were down at the seventy-five-foot level, which is well beyond my working depth. I haven't speared a fish at that depth since injuring my ears. After that painful experience, I'd given up on the idea of ever diving deep again, and changed my diving style to fit my limitations—though I admit to a fascination for making the deep dive.

There are two major obstructions that stand between the free diver and the depths. One is physical and the other is psychological, and they are interconnected. Simply put, the deeper the dive the stronger the legs must be to push up through the great weight of water pressing down from above. After a certain point, every foot becomes a millstone and sixty feet becomes a very long way from fifty feet. A diver who has made a dive to sixty feet is not going to ascend with the ease he did at twenty feet. Instead he rises several inches then returns to his original position. At that moment he realizes that a tremendous amount of strength and energy will be required to return him safely to the surface, and this at the end of the breath hold, when that strength and energy are at their lowest levels.

Experiencing this enormous weight of water for the first time leaves a deep and abiding impression on the breath hold diver. It is a tight, anxious feeling he is not eager to experience again. It creates tension which robs the breath hold, and tempers the will, if not the courage, to dive deeply. Overcoming these strong feelings that derive from our basic instincts for survival is difficult. Initially, the diver must force himself into a relaxed state at the edge of his personal depth level. Then he must carefully monitor his physical condition, which fluctuates due to fatigue and ocean conditions, and adjust his depth limits accordingly.

Bob Stanbery has observed that a free diver gains approximately ten feet of depth a year until he reaches his limit. Then he develops a style that best fits his working depth. Diving to depth is not a prerequisite for being a good blue water hunter; on the average, most hunters are able to comfortably work (dive down, stay down, stalk a fish, spear it, and return to the surface) depths of thirty-five to fifty feet. Beyond that the influence of depth comes increasingly into play.

A deep dive is dependent on several elements: one is the condition of the water. It is easier to dive deeper in clear water than in murky water;

good visibility makes the underwater terrain more accessible and it is psychologically easier to dive down to something you can see than something you cannot see. In clear water the diver can maintain visual contact with his surroundings and keep a surface-to-bottom perspective. In the cloudy, chilly water of the Pacific there is a feeling of depth and isolation. And the degree of light and temperature change that occurs every ten feet or so ominously reminds the diver that the great Pacific looms ever oppressive above him.

The powerful presence of the ocean hangs heavily on the diver who is trying to get all he can out of every dive. There is always a margin of time set aside for the return to the surface, but so much can and does happen on a dive that the margin is often cut paper thin. A significant number of hunters have experienced blackout at one time or another. Fortunately, there was usually another diver in the water who has pulled them to the surface and revived them. But not always; when competition hunting reached its height in popularity during the 60's, four Americans died on separate occasions, all presumably trying to extend their bottom times. I'm amazed that it doesn't happen more often.

There is a handful of divers who have pushed through these deep barriers and can work depths up to and beyond a hundred feet. Their bottom time ranges from a minute and a half to two minutes, so this ability is not due to abnormally large lung capacities. Performing this exceptional feat is as much psychological as physical, although all are obviously in top physical form. Somehow these divers are able to stay relaxed and within them-

selves while this great pressure bears down on
them from above. Art Pinder, Mike Wilkie, Jay
Riffe, John Ernst and Terry Maas are the Americans known to me who are able to make these
hundred-foot dives. If there are others, and there
are probably a few, it nonetheless remains a select group.

* * *

At the crack of dawn I'm out of my bunk, drink-
ing tea and wolfing down a handful of cookies. The
Low Now is dancing on her painter, anxious to
return to the rock. In twenty minutes we are
there, the kelp is up and we drift quietly into the
bed, coming to rest on top of the eastern plateau.
Before swimming out into the deep water, I make
a few preliminary dives to the bottom of the plateau in an attempt to build up some bottom time.
After two dives, I abandon the idea and move out
past the plateau where it drops off to the hundred and ten-foot bottom.

There is no kelp out here—crystal blue water,
fifty feet of visibility from the top with the blacksmiths silhouetted against the steep, angled rays
of the early morning sun. Swimming to their edge,
I peer down the sharp incline, looking for a spot
that will provide a good viewing position. There
is a light colored boulder that juts several feet
out from the incline at approximately fifty feet
and affords a clean drop into deeper water.

Pumping up, I drop down on four kicks and
glide. My left hand is fastened to my nose and I
make at least six pressure equalizations before
reaching the boulder. My right hand is on the new

speargun trailing the yellow poly line that marks my position. Settling down on the boulder, I'm tight and already feel the need for air. This is a far different world than the one twenty feet above my head, here the water is thicker, darker and several degrees colder; the bright colors have long been absorbed and all that remains are shades of browns and grays. To suppress my need for air I begin to count: a thousand one, a thousand two; if a fish were to pass by at this moment, it would be difficult to pursue it. The key to deep diving, to any free diving, is to remain relaxed and comfortable; on this first dive of the morning I am neither. A thousand thirty, long enough for a first dive, pushing hard off the boulder I kick toward the ceiling. The depth gives density to the water and it takes an extra effort just to move my legs back and forth to generate a strong enough pull to lift me off of the bottom. Putting my back to it, I slowly ascend, pushing up against the weight, feeling the ocean gradually release me.

Resting on the surface, I consider the probabilities for finding fish. There could be a white sea bass moving beneath me at this very moment. Even if I could see it from the surface, I couldn't dive to it until the oxygen level in my body has returned to normal. Any opportunities to spear a fish will have to come during the one minute stretch I spend on the boulder. The possibilities seem remote.

I hyperventilate and my lungs expand, taking in more air than before. After one last breath to capacity I drop down, gliding to the boulder. Twenty-five feet beneath me, large calico vibrate in the thermocline; when their curiosity about me is satisfied, they casually drift away, knowing they cannot be followed. My thoughts wander with them to the depths, and I must remind myself to stay alert and continue scanning the water. The need for air is constantly present, yet I wait until the last instant before pushing off, extending my bottom time with each dive.

After twenty minutes a good rhythm has developed; pumping up, kicking down, equalizing, gliding to the boulder, then resting and regaining my breath. Another half hour passes and I feel at ease with the depth and enjoy making the dives. It is exhilarating to break through those internal and external barriers and probe new territory.

Down again on the boulder, waiting, watching and as I look, a white sea bass absolutely materializes before my eyes, and it is a monster—over sixty pounds. I move off the boulder and glide down toward it. The white senses me almost immediately and changes direction, dipping in the direction of the bottom. Already past seventy feet, I continue to drop. My ears are in pain, but I cannot risk moving my hand to my nose to equalize for fear the fish might spook at the movement or sound. At eighty feet I close to within twenty feet of the fish; it is almost on the bottom and I'm well beyond my depth limit. As I line up for the shot the white reads my intentions and turns, taking away its broadsides. I'm quickly losing any chance for a good shot so I aim slightly high to compensate for the distance and release the arrow. It sails high of the fish, nicking the dorsal fin. I clear my ears and start pulling for the surface, which is now a moon's distance away. Keeping my head down, I concentrate on steady, powerful kicks, my legs moving to full extension, pushing up to the light. Reaching the surface, heaving in fresh air, my breathing dominates my body. After resting for a long while, I haul up the line. The sight of the arrow with the detached tip dangling harmlessly at its end punctuates my disappointment. That was the largest white sea bass I've seen in ten years. Any chance of seeing a fish that size again is zero. That was it, one opportunity every ten years. Though ten years from now, a fish of that size will no longer exist in these waters, and in all likelihood neither will I.

Back in the early 70's I missed an easy shot on a white sea bass that was over a hundred pounds. Al came across a hundred-pounder that was sleeping in the kelp. He backed off, took his time, and missed the fish. These big ones have a lot of magic—maybe it's just not possible. Yas Ikeda landed the largest white sea bass taken by spear, at seventy-seven pounds. Yas must have had some magic of his own that day. That was a long time ago, and the fish have been getting smaller every year. No one has come close to the big fish that were taken a decade ago, and only a few keep trying.

I dive the boulder for another hour, once following a smaller white sea bass down to eighty feet before losing it to the bottom. The ascent is difficult and I struggle to the surface. The kick has been sucked out of my legs from the morning's workout. Realizing that I've nothing left, I paddle back to the *Low Now*.

Several years ago Al and Bob Donnell were hunting blacks at Anacapa Island, which is north of Los Angeles and south of Santa Barbara. Al got

into one; the fish sounded and wrapped around a
small reef in what was close to a hundred feet of
water. Al is not a deep diver and Bob, who can
work a respectable depth, still does not fall into
that select group with Ernst, Maas and the others. Neither Al nor Bob could make the dive to
that depth, locate the line and free it up from every crack and crevice it had worked its way into,
and then return to the surface. So they devised a
plan: first one diver would drop down to the bottom and start working the line free. The other
diver would stay on the surface and count, a thousand one, a thousand two, etc., until he reached
sixty, then he would dive down to sixty feet and
catch the deep diver and kick them both to the
surface. They would rest then switch positions.
This tactic is similar to the fellow who jumped
out of an airplane without a parachute, depending on another jumper to follow him out with a
chute he could put on during free fall. If the surface diver is not where he should be or the deep
diver cannot locate him in the hazy water, the
deep diver probably drowns. Al and Bob continued to dive in this fashion until the line was freed
and the fish boated.

**

I'm in the water a half hour earlier than yesterday and expect to be rewarded for my sacrifice.
Moving out past the kelp, I spy those same big
calicos hovering around the same kelp stalk; another board meeting breaks up when they see me
approach. Much of yesterday's visibility is gone, a
current is running and there are half a dozen sea

lions cavorting around the boulder. The only posi-
tive thing going for me this morning is that I know
the fish are here.

The blacksmiths are the only familiar sign left
over from yesterday and they are accompanied by
a school of anchovies busily weaving a silver pattern of light close to the surface. I work the boulder for forty minutes, the current putting an additional strain on the dives, and the sea lions all
around me bring their form of chaos to the area.
Eventually, they force me to move north two hundred feet where another rock outcropping extends
beyond the incline in forty-five feet of water.

My second dive on this new position finds a cormorant foraging on the seaweed-covered rocks
twenty feet away. Curious, I swim over to this deep
diving bird and it quickly shoots for the surface.
Swimming hard, I chase it to the top. Easily beating me, it releases a load of duck crap on the way.
I receive its message loud and clear and pop
through the ceiling only seconds after the cormorant, and watch it scurry across the surface and
become airborne. Here is an evolutionary marvel
that has adapted to two entirely different envi-
ronments. A deep diver of the seas and a pilot of
the skies concealed in an awkward looking bird
that few give a second look. I watch with envy until
it becomes a speck in the distance.

This new location is dead. Even the bait fish
refuse to swim through, so I move back to my original boulder and dive another twenty minutes. The
conditions are deteriorating and my one sided
conversation begins: "This is my last dive", "Just
one more", etc. Down again on the boulder and
staring out into the gloomy blue, two barely dis-

cernible shadows are outlined against the haze and I drop down to intercept. The distance between us is too great and the whites drift off and disappear into the bottom. Fatigued from the deep dives, I declare the sighting to be enough for the day and return to the *Low Now*. The weekend is coming up so I'll stay out of the water until Monday or Tuesday. Hopefully the visibility will improve, the current will subside, and the sea lions will go elsewhere for their morning workout.

The weekend brings sunshine, an armada of boats from the mainland and some tightness in my left ear. My time on board is spent sanding the tissues of the *Infinity* down for the umpteenth time and watching the various boats come into the cove seeking an anchorage for their two-day stay. Observing this same scene each weekend I've come to be a fair judge of sailors by the way they anchor their boats. Anchoring is a skill that is often taken lightly until near calamity marks the value of knowing how to do it properly. Those who have difficulty with it have both my sympathy and attention; they are a potential hazard to the *Infinity*. When I think I've seen it all, from losing anchor lines to dragging anchors, to fouling props, to drifting helplessly into other boats, a new twist is thrown in and keeps each weekend interesting.

Last Saturday afternoon brought the best act of the summer: two fellows skippering a twenty-five-foot sloop are looking for a spot to settle for the night. They attempt to anchor close to the cliffs on my port side, but cannot get a firm bite on the rocky bottom. Several times they came dangerously close to the submerged rocks that lie close to shore. I offered some suggestions, but they would have none of it. Twice they drifted across my stern line and I had to play it out so it wouldn't foul in their prop. Their determination to anchor close to shore finally became their undoing and they put their boat up on one of the submerged rocks with a thud, the sloop coming to rest on the port side of its hull. Jumping into the *Low Now,* I tied a line to their bow cleat and waited for the surge to give the boat a lift, then pulled them off the rock. Before I could return to the *Infinity* they backed over its stern line, this time fouling it around their prop and unbeknownst to me, nearly cutting the line in two. When they freed up the line, I suggested, in the same clear style of the cormorant, that they anchor on my starboard side. The bottom there is sandy, they would have more room to maneuver and more importantly, it would take them off my windward side. They blundered about for another thirty minutes before giving up and moving on. If there was ever a floating disaster looking for a place to happen, it was these two. Actually, they were likeable in their ineptness and as I watched them go, I thanked them for the entertaining afternoon. Before returning to the cabin I noticed that the *Infinity* was a bit out of position; the nearly severed anchor line broke when I cinched it up, casting the stern adrift and bringing the curtain down on the final act of this early evening comedy.

Tuesday morning, I'm in the water as the sun lifts from it. The day is clear and already warm, the sea lions are dozing on the rock, pushed deeper into their dreamless sleep by the warming sun. The current is light yet restless, and I'm afraid it will not be long before it picks up momentum. The visibility has improved over Friday and I glide to my familiar boulder with comfortable ease. I work the boulder for an hour, moving at a steady pace, down for a minute and a half and up for two minutes, but see no sign of fish.

The current starts to pick up and as it does the visibility drops. After diving another thirty minutes, the area begins to close down entirely. "One more dive," I say, then do one more and one more after that. The current will push the fish down, my ear feels tight. "Why am I doing this?" On the way up from the tenth "last dive" a yellowtail, a big one, close to forty pounds, appears before me. We are at the same depth. The fish swaggers by fifteen feet away and I let the spear fly then break for the surface.

These big yellows are powerful, more powerful than a white sea bass the same size, and it storms off with a rush. By the time I reach the top and get a firm hold on the line, the fish has emptied a third of the reel. Kicking hard and maintaining tension on the line, I gain no ground, but neither does the fish. Suddenly the yellow starts moving erratically; one of the sea lions, very large, well over two hundred pounds, is attacking the fish. I watch the drama unfold from the surface; the sea lion is determined and gets hold of the yellow— biting its back just behind the dorsal fin—and tries to swim off with it, but the yellow is too big and too strong and powers out of the sea lion's mouth. The chase continues: the sea lion has it again, and again the yellow powers away. If this continues I could easily lose the fish. Anything could happen, the tip could be pulled out by the additional stress on the spear point, or the fish, tiring, could eventually be subdued by the sea lion. Diving down the line, I come to the fish, but cannot get my hands on it. It is swimming in a tight circled frenzy with me holding one end of the line. The sea lion lunges for another bite and I try to kick it away. It comes around behind me to the other side and the yellow swims away from it, looping the line around my leg just below the knee and cinching it tight. Holding the loose part of my end of the line I try to unwind from this dangerous situation, but the fish is frantic and pulls hard against the line. A rush of adrenaline uses what is left of my air and I yank on the line to no avail: it is too tight. The sea lion moves in again and the fish swims back to my other side. In that moment there is some slack and I free the line from my leg and pump for the surface. Back on top I try to pull the fish up to me, but the sea lion has a firm bite on the tiring fish as it's swimming off with it. Pulling on the line keeps the two close, but I'm losing the battle. Dropping down the line again and pulling on it at the same time, I reach the sea lion, give it a kick in the neck and it drops the fish. Grabbing the arrow, I work my way up to the fish getting hold of its tail, then slip a hand in its gills. The sea lion is not about to let this easy meal get away and comes right into me looking for a piece of the yellow. I'm able to push it away with my foot while moving toward the surface. It swims to within arm's length of me, never taking its eyes off of the fish. Near the surface a blue shark blows by fifty feet away; with all of this commotion it comes with no surprise. When I reach the surface the shark has disappeared, but the sea

lion is with me and stays with me until I've de-
posited the yellow into the *Low Now*. Only then
does it accept defeat and swim away.

9

"EATERS"

As was noted earlier, the shark, among all of the ocean's creatures, has been singularly responsible for keeping man's undersea activities confined to the shallows of his shoreline. Our obsession with the shark's potential for killing is equal to our fascination with the specter of death itself. In fact the words "death" and "shark" carry the same impact and bear the same implication. The shark is portrayed as the most deliberate killer in nature; a silently efficient, unthinking, unfeeling and almost unkillable animal. It represents the last omnipotent creaturely threat to man that springs from the natural world.

For 99 percent of the SCUBA divers and other lovers of the oceans the shark is a threat that is rarely seen much less experienced; for the blue water hunter the shark is a profound reality. Yet the hunter initially moves out into the blue water filled with the same fearful information that

has been fed to all of society. He is not immune to
the books and movies or to the stories, real or fabricated, of attacks on humans by sharks. He has
been conditioned, like everyone else, to react with
terror at the sight of a shark, particularly if he is
in the water with one. The blue water hunter can
only move so far into the ocean before this psy-
chic weight becomes so great that it must be removed before he can truly become an ocean
hunter. This release from the shark is a process
that almost every hunter has undergone. I say almost every hunter, because some never complete
this exorcism, and there are a few who have nothing to exorcise.

The process begins, at least it did for me, with
an encounter with the devil himself. I'd been diving blue water for almost two years and was filled
to the brim with those culturally induced fears.
One eye looked for fish, while the other attempted
to pierce the impenetrable blue looking for "eat-
ers," as the tribe likes to call them. I had speared
a yellowtail off of Pukey Point at the Coronado
islands, out of San Diego in Mexican waters, and
as I worked the fish to me a ten-foot dusky, one of
the few aggressive sharks in these waters,
stormed in and hit the yellowtail just behind the
pectoral fin, violently tearing off the body, and
swam away. The speed and ferociousness of the
assault was everything the films depicted, and I
unwittingly transferred the scene onto myself. The
dusky graphically demonstrated what I had long
felt, that man is woefully vulnerable in the ocean.

That vulnerability and the realization of it are
among the primary reasons why there are so few
blue water hunters. As the race car driver must

accept the hard reality of an accident in a race, the blue water hunter must accept his vulnerability in the ocean. But there the similarity ends because the racer does not have the time to think about an accident; he is fully occupied with driving the car. The hunter has plenty of time to think. He thinks about the speared fish and how the bloody and frenzied movement calls out to whatever lies lurking beyond his range of vision. He ponders his slow movements while traveling from the surface to the depths and back, knowing he moves like a sick or wounded seal. He is acutely aware that he would be unable to flee or hide from an attacking shark in the improbable event he were given the chance. He carries into this alien environment nothing more than a bow and arrow with which he must protect himself against a prehistoric beast whose overpowering size, strength and maneuverability only further accentuate his glaring inadequacies in the ocean.

The dusky swam in my thoughts for a long time. I couldn't bury the scene of it tearing into the yellowtail. This preoccupation eroded my concentration and stole the joy that comes with blue water hunting. I hoped that in time the shark would fade and I'd feel as free in the deep water as I was in the kelp beds. But it did not leave me and I felt its weight whenever I moved into bottomless water. Over the next year I carried that dusky until the excess weight of it started to drown me. The only escape from a situation that was getting worse instead of better was a clear and final decision: either I must release the shark completely or quit diving and do something else.

To give up diving was unthinkable. I had to pry

myself loose from the shackles of the dusky. The first step was to accept my vulnerability in the ocean, that is, clearly accept the reality of it without the influence of fear that muddies the water and feeds the terror. In that full acceptance lies a certain freedom; a new space is created where there is room to maneuver, or defend, or even attack, if necessary, much the same as the full acceptance of death alters the view of life and brings a certain luster and richness to it that was not there before. Secondly, I had to erase from my mind all images of sharks that my imagination conjured. That was the key; when the sharks began to filter into my head I'd block them out by focusing on the ocean before me. It was not easy at first, but it soon became habit, and eventually my mind cleared itself of its dark wanderings, and my freedom was nearly complete.

As thoughts of the shark faded, the ocean opened up to a new and broader view. My concentration improved and my hunting skills followed; soon my kinship with the blue water became equal to that of the kelp beds. Slightly less than a year after this conversion, an incident occurred that became my final liberation from the shark.

It was during my second trip to Guardian Angel Island. I had just speared a large grouper. The fish had holed up in sixty feet of water. Diving to the cave, I hung at the entrance trying to determine the best way to pull the grouper out. Suddenly and very clearly I felt another presence in the water and turned in response. Behind me, twenty feet away, was the largest shark I'd ever seen before or since in the water, with the exception of the whale shark. Face to face it was huge, a yard wide in the head and eighteen feet in length. It is difficult to judge the weight of a creature of this size; a guess would be somewhere between fifteen hundred and two thousand pounds. It hung motionless in the water with all the confidence of an old despot.

While the shark's great power was oozing through its skin, my speargun stock was floating on the surface. Out of breath, I ascended; it was a vulnerable moment. The shark made no move toward me, and when I reached the top it swam lazily off and out of sight.

After resting for five minutes I dropped back down to the holed up grouper. The fish had worked its way deeper into the cave and as I tugged away on it that same feeling came over me again, clear and clean as though being gently but firmly informed that something was about. Turning, I found the same shark ten feet behind me. Dropping the line to the fish I made a half threatening pass, empty handed. It was a weak gesture and the shark did not move an inch. Needing air, I pushed off the bottom and began to kick my way up. As I did the shark moved into me. Kicking harder, I rose above it and as I did it swam directly beneath me, so close that I had to lift my fins to keep from hitting its massive dorsal fin. When I reached the surface the shark turned and came back toward me. Considering its size, I couldn't interpret this move as anything less than aggressive.

Spotting the anchored boat a hundred yards away, I swam to it, keeping an eye on the shark as best I could until it broke contact with me. Fifteen minutes later four of us returned and buzzed the area in the boat, then several hunters rode shotgun for me while I retrieved the grouper. The shark made one last fleeting appearance and then was gone.

Sensing the shark was not my first evidence that it is possible for man, if he is in the right frame of mind, to allow the stronger signals within the ocean to penetrate his consciousness. I've seen it work regularly when hunting for fish. So strong was the shark's unseen presence that I've come to trust this form of sensing completely and have surrendered myself to that process.

My belief has been regularly reinforced by my experience over the years and I've had no "surprise" confrontations. Maybe I'm just lucky, but I can't help but believe that it may be one's attitude about sharks more than anything else which influences an encounter. No one can say for sure what draws sharks to a diver; sometimes it's just bad luck. Those few hunters I know who handle their dread of sharks by repressing their fears and masking them in bravado and bold talk always seem to have more encounters than those who are or have managed to become relatively fearless in the ocean.

The single shark incident that had the strongest impact on the tribe began, for me, on a white sea bass hunt down at the Coronados with Frank Taylor and Wes Andrews of San Diego. It was during the spring of '73 and the white sea bass were running strong. Frank had been out the day before and saw huge schools of whites, landing several. He called me and the next day the three of us went out to South Island and dove the Middle Grounds. The dive was unforgettable because it was the last time I saw one of the grand schools of white sea bass on the move. Diving down into fifty feet of visibility I looked out into an iridescent wall of movement, a shimmering mass of reflected silver light that stood thirty feet high and went fifty feet across. Hundreds of fish, each forty pounds or more, crossed in front of me. I cling to that moment as though it were a personal responsibility to recall every detail of my final look into the Pacific past.

Both Wes and I each received a handsome white sea bass and on our way back to the mainland he told me of his plan. Wes wanted to assemble four or five of the best spearfishermen in this part of the country and take a long range boat trip down to Guadalupe island, which lies two hundred miles southwest of San Diego, in Mexican waters. The idea was to hunt for tuna, the supreme challenge for the blue water spearfisherman. The tuna's speed and power are unmatched in the ocean and landing one of any size is a rare feat. It has been done, but not often. Ron Merker, an outstanding white sea bass hunter in the 60's, speared the largest bluefin tuna, fifty seven pounds, at Guadalupe in September of '62, and no one has come close to it in over a decade.

Wes asked me to come along and organize the trip from my end. Returning to Los Angeles I contacted Bob Stanbery, whom I knew would be interested, and shifted my organizing responsibilities to him. A month before the trip I had to bow out because I couldn't get the time off from my job. On that same weekend Al and I were hunting for white sea bass down the coast in Oceanside, and I told him that my spot on the trip would be open, and to contact Bob if he was interested. He

was, and he was able to take his young son, Al Jr.,
along for the ride.

***

The boat arrived at Guadalupe on schedule in
the late afternoon and of course the divers wanted
to do some scouting before dark; nothing serious,
just enough to get a feel for the water and see
how this new territory shaped up. The boat was
anchored in a protected cove for the evening, and
as the sun set all divers had returned to the boat
with no reported fish sightings, except Al, who
had not yet come back but was in sight of the boat.
Wes was in his street clothes back on the fantail
when he heard Al yell, "Tourniquet," and saw the
blood in the water. Immediately the skipper
dropped the bow anchor and they backed the boat
up to Al, who was floating in the water without
his weight belt, mask or speargun. He was uncon-
scious when they pulled him aboard; he had been
bitten in the calf and his femoral artery severed.
Al momentarily regained consciousness, then
lapsed into a coma and died shortly after from
loss of blood.

Although Al's was the first fatality of a blue
water hunter from a shark attack in the Pacific,
his death rumbled through the tribe like a terrible shock wave. His loss struck deep and became
a lasting reminder of the vulnerability each diver
faces in the ocean. If it could happen to the best,
it could happen to anyone. A portion of the shark's
tooth was found imbedded in Al's ankle bone. It
was removed and examined; it had come from the
mouth of a great white shark.

10

BLUE SKIES, EMPTY SEAS

The last dives at Ship Rock were more than my ears could bear. Under the constant pressure both middle ears filled with fluid. I stayed out of the water for a week and finished up the last of the sanding and varnishing on the *Infinity*. During the second week I only dove in shallow water. The cheerful kelp forests recaptured my interest and I exchanged my speargun for a camera. By the end of the third week I had lost all motivation to hunt for game fish. I began to enjoy my visits into the kelp beds and my eye, no longer the hunter's eye, sought light, form and texture rather than movement. And the hunter's alertness gave way to the relaxed carefree manner of the food gatherer who satisfies himself with the light work of scouring a reefy bottom for scallop, abalone and lobster, content to eat peanut butter sandwiches when the forage is unproductive.

It is now late in the summer and this life fits like an old jacket. I've done all the work I can do on the *Infinity* and my existence is reduced to sleeping, eating, taking pictures, and gathering food. Each day holds itself apart from the last.

Changes occur continually; the wind fluctuates, the current is up and it is down and I remain reasonably fixed in the center of it all. Through these months I've been very high and very low and everywhere in between. I've managed it all and know what to expect from the boat and from myself. If the *Infinity* breaks, I fix her; if the visibility is poor today, it will be diveable tomorrow. I take the given without resistance and accept the inconveniences that come with this kind of living (I ran out of my store of fresh water some time ago and must fill two four-gallon buckets with each trip I make to the *Isthmus*).

In the morning I rise and read the day as if it were my newspaper; the wind speaks its many tongues as it whistles through the stays, each sound and every change in pitch revealing its disposition. The creaking joints of the rolling *Infinity* report the character of the ocean and transmit the messages up through her hull and into my legs. Her movement is my movement, and she is alive with sound. The currents express their power through the anchor lines and are readily disclosed by the sound of a tightening line. I am connected to the boat and the boat to the sea and the messages breathe me in and breathe me out.

Several weeks pass and I blissfully continue to take pictures and scrounge for an evening meal. One day, returning from the *Isthmus* with a load of fresh water I run over to Ship rock and look over the present conditions. The water is crystal clear, sixty to seventy feet, the kelp is straight up, and the sight of it revives the sleeping hunter. Returning to the *Infinity* and suiting up, I bounce back to the rock to renew my pursuit of white sea

bass. The blacksmiths are still there, and the water is perfect for hunting. Three straight days I
dive the rock without seeing a fish, then it occurs
to me that this is the second week in September.
The white sea bass rarely stay in these waters
later than mid-August, and usually they have mi-
grated north by the end of July.

Now I understand that when the white sea bass
continued north to their spawning grounds the
hunter in me left with them.

And now the white sea bass are on their way to
a destination that so far has eluded man and the
great arm of technology that can lift the thin blue
blanket covering the ocean and reduce the wild
creatures below to blips on a screen. It is one of
life's small miracles that somewhere north of
Catalina and south of San Francisco the white sea
bass are able to spawn unmolested by us.

The spawning grounds are the last refuge for
the white sea bass. Between those grounds and
the Pacific waters off Mexico, the white sea bass
live a dangerous existence. In the path of their
annual migration from the southern waters off the
Baja peninsula up along the California coast lies
every imaginable fishing device, from the most
primitive net to the state-of-the-art in fishing
technology. Mexican gill nets run the length of
their coastline and are virtually unregulated. They
take everything that passes through. Every gill
netter should see the horror of a gill net at work
underwater. In the midst of this ever-moving and
life-filled environment lies a web of death, with
fish of many species caught and struggling, dying
or already dead by suffocation. The contrast between the living ocean and the deathly stillness

of a gill net numbs the mind.

The white sea bass that manage to elude the maze of gill nets in Mexican waters have just begun their perilous journey. When they reach the United States they find that man here is equally deadly and vastly more efficient. Single engine planes fly above the stretches of kelp that run intermittently along the entire length of the Baja peninsula and the California coast. They search out dark areas in the water that mark a school of fish. When one is located the plane radios a nearby fishing vessel with the bearings, and the boat proceeds to wrap the entire school. The white sea bass must encounter this country's most advanced fishing methods before they reach their spawning grounds in northern waters.

There are no limits. The commercial boats take everything they can lay their hands on, and each year the fleets weigh their tonnage and the industry announces whether it has been a good year or a bad one. In either case they keep on taking. The irony is that for all the millions of tons of fish that the fishing industry pulls out of the water every year, they never see the empty space that is left when the fish are gone. It is a bottomless well for them, the last horn of plenty, and like the men of the land, they will continue to squeeze until all the wild life in the oceans is gone.

The tribe is solitary witness to the slaughter; they alone have seen the empty space once filled by the pelagic fish of the Pacific and the grouper of the Gulf. The fathers were able to see the ocean wilderness as it existed virtually untouched by man since Creation, and they were watching when man began to dip his giant hand into these life-giving waters. The second generation was permitted their fleeting look into the past and saw the great schools roam the depth as great herds once walked the plains. Like the last tribes of the plains who witnessed the decimation of the wildlife, the second generation looked on as the great schools diminished into groups of twos and threes and the giant leaders vanished altogether, leaving the adolescents to lead what is left to the spawning grounds.

Last year Terry Maas flew down the coast of Baja in a light plane in an attempt to locate the kelp bed that was said to hold the last of the big schools of white sea bass. He found the bed, took his bearings, and returned home to plan his strategy. Terry decided to wait until winter when he was sure the fish would be in those southerly waters. He returned by car, and it was a typical Baja trip for him and his partner, Jim Mabry. The highway was worn and potholed and it took the better part of a day to go forty miles on an uncharted dirt road which ended on top of a two hundred-foot-high cliff that overlooked the Pacific.

Using ropes, they lowered their gear: an inflatable boat, engine, gasoline, dive gear, food and themselves down the sheer cliffs. The following morning they reassembled the boat and headed out into a formidable surf. Finding the kelp bed, which was seven miles off the coast, was difficult and took most of the morning. They dove hard until dark, and did not see a fish. The trip was a bust, and it symbolized the last major effort to find the vanishing white sea bass. The great schools were no more. Returning home, Terry and Jim knew they were closing in on the final gasp, not just for the white sea bass, but for themselves as well. On the drive back the conversation drifted to the last remaining hunting grounds and the unmentionable was re-examined: a possible trip to Guadalupe island and the ultimate fish, the blue-fin tuna. It was still there waiting and the rumors of the bluefin have remained rumors. Only Ron Merker's achievement twenty years past stands as evidence to what might be found.

The waters of Guadalupe and the deep Pacific are not the same blue waters that lie outside the kelp beds or the deeper waters of Ship rock. These are the purple blue waters of the vast Pacific.

***

During the early seventies, before Al's death, there was a movement by the tribe out into the purple waters and one summer afternoon, I dove the Catalina channel hunting for albacore. The water is three to five thousand feet deep and I felt like a grain of sand suspended in a blue chamber with walls I could never reach. The endlessness of it seemed to be pressing in with a force that made me feel small and vulnerable. At least in the waters outside the kelp I can know where danger might be coming from. In the Gulf, reefs and rocky bottoms offer the illusion of safety, but out here there was nothing, a great nothingness that seemed bent on absorbing everything that entered into its blue tissues. Anything could come from anywhere; top, bottom and from every side. I didn't know where to look for fish or how to see. I strained my eyes within this sapphire jewel, waiting for a school of those missile-like fish to appear, knowing I had only seconds for an opportunity to shoot before it disappeared through the invisible walls in the opposite direction. With no visual reference points in this clear water, accurate perception was difficult and distorted, leaving me disoriented. And with disorientation in five thousand feet of water came the feeling of vulnerability. The sharks out here are not the sharks that sniff about the coast at night scavenging the already dead for their meals, nor the ones I had reconciled within the hollows of my mind. These are the large and far more aggressive sharks of the fathomless depth that prey on the powerful tuna and are quick to respond to weakness in other ocean creatures. I saw no albacore that day and found no reason to return to the purple blue again.

Save for a few exceptions, the movement out into the deep Pacific ended in '73 with Al's death. Were it not for the diminishing fish and the prospects of an empty sea the tribe might never have thought to return ten years later.

While Terry and Jim were drawing up their plans to dive Guadalupe, another contingent of hunters had already begun to push out onto the purple edge. In the 60's Jim Baldwin became one of the top competitive divers in the country. He abandoned competition as that era of diving folded in the seventies and turned his considerable energies to blue water hunting. He also turned a small real estate development company into a multi-million dollar holding. Jim spends a good deal of his money and most of his free time in the pursuit of big fish.

Five years ago Jim bought a sixty-seven-foot

cruising yacht, the *Blue Dolphin*, and outfitted it with the latest in electronic fish monitoring equipment. Joining Jim were some of the best free diving spearfishermen in the country: Jay Riffe, Dick Glenn, Mike Wilkie, George Kuznecovs, Bob Caruso and George Meyers.

The first few years the *Blue Dolphin* and its crew hunted the farther reaches of the Gulf, areas so remote that without Jim's boat and equipment, the tribe could not reach them. In their excursions down the Pacific, the deeper waters began to lure them away from the grouper and into this new territory with its untried fish.

Last fall the crew of the *Blue Dolphin* made their first determined effort to hunt the deep Pacific. To hear Jim describe the experience is like listening to a novice diver speak of his first impressions of the ocean.

"It's a completely different world out there. It takes a week to adjust to the water; it's so clear, and with no reference points the eyes can't make an accurate fix. There could be a current running and you have no sense of it. The sharks are an oversized reality and swim in your mind like background noise that is never turned off."

They headed south fifteen to twenty miles off shore down the Pacific side of the Baja peninsula in water several thousand feet deep, tracking the bottom for pinnacles. When a high point appeared on the Fathometer several divers would jump in and scout the area for fish. After several shark incidents, and one in particular that produced thirty to forty sharks, they changed their procedure to first explore the pinnacles using SCUBA, and if the water was not shark-infested, they would free dive it. Diving down to the top of the pinnacles on a breath hold, they would hang above them in the liquid sky and wait for fish. They saw schools of amberjack and yellowtail and let them pass. They were looking specifically for wahoo and dorado, sometimes called dolphinfish or mahi mahi. Wahoo is similar to an oversized barracuda and can weigh as much as a hundred pounds. It is a deep water predator in the strictest sense. The elusive dorado is very quick and swims with darting movements. It is difficult to get close to and so is rarely speared.

At the first sighting of a wahoo Jim watches it slink into view with no apparent tail or body movement, a torpedo launched at birth whose target is anything that swims.

"I had the distinct feeling that the fish was stalking me." They were both stalking one another.

"The fish took its time moving in, until it seemed to be right on top of me, then taking deliberate aim at this point blank range, I pulled the trigger —and watched the arrow fall ten feet short of the fish."

The divers constantly experimented with their stalking techniques, trying to get closer to the fish. By the second week they had begun to adjust to the environment and Jim worked his way in for a good shot on a wahoo.

"I waited until it seemed I could touch the fish with my hand. It looked enormous, but there was no way of gauging its size. When I released the arrow it struck the fish solidly and the wahoo tore away with such force that I could barely hold on to the trailing line. The fish was bouncing me through the water at close to ten miles an hour."

In the first five minutes Jim was dragged over half a mile. For the next twenty minutes the fish maintained the same power before starting to tire. The chase boat stayed right with Jim and fortunately, no sharks appeared. After forty minutes the fish was boated and at eighty pounds, the largest ever speared.

The hunters continued to feel out the water for another week, all making the same adjustment that Jim had made earlier. Eventually Jay speared another record fish, the largest dorado ever taken by a free diver.

The crew of the *Blue Dolphin* had broken through the purple wall and emerged on the last ocean frontier. By their own admission they never reached the level of comfort that they enjoyed closer to the coast, but they could nevertheless as hunters function in this alien wilderness. They had entered the farthest outpost of a wild kingdom armed with a primitive hunting tool and had acquired food. They acknowledged the primal human self, the hunter who lies inside the civilized skin in all men. Genetically we are still very much the hunters who trekked the earth until an evolutionary breath ago. Our ancestors survived for four million years in the center of the wilderness. Then in a few short strides man tamed the land and in the doing, tamed himself. But the fierceness that sustained him in the wilds is still very much alive, held in silent abeyance, a smoldering fire that burns inwardly, devouring man with the suppressed rage of an ancient beast whose time has passed, yet who can never sleep peacefully.

* * *

Terry had a fair idea of what might lie before him at Guadalupe island, and in his preparation he flew to Hawaii the preceding spring and tested the water sixteen miles off of the Kona coast. There he and fellow divers, Terry Lentz and Dennis Okada of Hawaii, dove a fish aggregation buoy that is as large as a two-car garage and is anchored in thousands of feet of water and suspended sixty feet from the surface. Tuna and other deep water fish congregate around this underwater island in the middle of the Pacific, and Terry wanted to acquire some firsthand experience with tuna in crystal clear water.

They cut ten pounds of squid into bite-sized chunks and packed them into a half a dozen plastic bags. Opening a bag underwater, they let the contents drift down to the buoy on the strong current. Large sharks in the vicinity forced the divers into a team: one diver handles the bag of chum; the second diver carries a bang stick to ward off sharks; the third is the shooter. They could see large yellowfin tuna hanging near the buoy as the squid chunks spread to a diameter of fifty feet and drifted toward the fish. As the tuna began to feed, the shooter dropped into the middle of the chum.

"These fish swim fifty-five miles an hour and they came in so fast, sucking in the chum in a feeding frenzy, that a clear shot was impossible."

All Terry could do was hold the speargun in one position and hope that the fish would swim in front of it. When it did, his reaction time could not keep pace with the flying tuna and he missed dead on shots. Eventually he speared a small three pounder, and Dennis hit a large one that easily broke loose from the arrow. (The combination of

the tuna's soft flesh and its tremendous power call
for precise placement of the arrow. It must either
penetrate the head, which is most difficult because
the fish is moving so rapidly, or strike the backbone, which would severely injure it as well as
give the spear point something solid to hang on
to.) After several unsuccessful runs, a large shark
moved into the area and forced the three out of
the water.

Terry stayed a week in Hawaii, attempting in
that brief period to acclimate himself to the clear
water. He never mentioned it, but there had to be
another acclimation process taking place. He and
Al had been close friends and the prospect of diving Guadalupe a decade after the death to hunt
the same fish must have lain uneasily in the back
of Terry's mind.

***

It is the middle of September, and while I take
pictures in the kelp beds of Catalina, Terry is eas-
ing himself over the side of the chase boat and
sees for the first time the waters of the Guadalupe
islands.

"The visibility is in excess of a hundred feet and
I can see schools of yellowtail that stretch in thin
lines for an eternity."

That first sight tells Terry he is in the center of
a thriving ocean, what the marine biologists call
a transition zone; an area where large concentra-
tions of pelagics pass through in their migrations
up and down the Pacific.

"The endless visibility and severe dropoffs give
the impression that we are dangling over the edge

of the earth. The unfamiliarity of this territory, combined with the knowledge that great whites frequent this area, make relaxation difficult."

But the divers who form this group are experienced, and after the first morning dive they begin to relax and find their pace. They read the actions of the bait fish, see the peaks and valleys that trail off beneath the rock islands, and register the points of interest that hold the territorial fish.

"We are hunting in every dimension," says Terry, "up, down and all around. Every eye strains to extend its reach in already disorienting water where we are suspended. My technique is to mingle with the bait fish which congregate forty to sixty feet down and to remain as still as possible. My first priority is to maintain my relaxation and block out the fact that these are the fastest, most powerful fish in the oceans. They can feel any tension that I emit, and like other blue water predators, will stay away from the diver when they sense it. If visual contact is made, I'll try and lure the fish to me in the same way I would attract a yellowtail."

Up and down, up and down they work, in that long and tiring dance that is the blue water hunter's. Then late in the afternoon, Terry draws in the first tuna.

"It was like seeing a small iridescent car moving through the water. It moved without any apparent tail or fin movement, one of them most thrilling moments I've ever experienced in the water."

The tuna swims close enough for a shot and Terry makes a good one, but the speed and distance of the fish fool him and the arrow strikes past mid-body. The tuna accelerates away at break-neck speed and the tip of the arrow pulls out.

Twenty minutes later Terry is hanging off the same pinnacle when a string of bluefin roll in. "In ultra slow movements I drift out of the bait to intercept the school at their mid-point. Instead of trying to pick out a particular fish, I wait until one crosses the elevation of my speargun."

One does and again Terry lets an arrow fly. This time it strikes close to the fish's head and the tuna thunders off, disappearing in an instant. "I reach the surface and yell for the chase boat. Despite the double-floated line with an attached sea an-chor, I am towed through the water at a tremen-dous speed. At one point the fish makes a large circle and I catch up to it and look down to see fifty to a hundred tuna, all about the same size as the one I've speared, hovering in the water. The backs of the fish are a foot and half wide and the water beneath me is gray with the backs of tuna. It is the most primitive, exciting spectacle a man could ever see."

The shot is well placed and after a half hour fight, Chuck Cook puts a second arrow into the fish and along with Lance Valencia, they finally subdue the bluefin, which weighed a hundred and eighty pounds.

The next two and half days every diver sees tuna and many take shots, but their arrows fall short. The water is too new and different for the major-ity of hunters and they don't have enough time to adjust to it. Jim Mabry and Gary Thompson are each able to put an arrow into a tuna, only to lose it when the fish accelerates off at blinding speed.

Terry said later, "The way the fish move in and out of sight in the twinkling of an eye gave the impression to many that these were apparitions, giant blue iridescent ghosts that appear on top of you, and when you shoot an arrow it falls twenty feet short and the tuna vanishes."

On the last day of their brief trip, in a four-foot wind chop and strong currents, Terry is making his final dives. He has found another location where small bait fish are congregating and "the place just feels right." While down on one of his dives and hanging with the bait, he looks to the surface and sees a school of fifty-pound tuna lolling in the swells, "but for all of my maneuvering, I can't draw them down to me."

At the forty-foot level on his fifth dive and vainly trying to bring in the surface tuna, Terry catches movement in the water beneath him. "I watch mesmerized as two bluefin of mammoth proportions head up from the endless bottom. Turning slightly away from the tuna piques their curiosity and draws them nearer. At their closest point they begin to angle away and as they do, I let go of my arrow."

Terry's placement of the shot turns out to be nothing less than miraculous. The arrow hits the backbone of the lead tuna, severely wounding it. A few inches higher or lower and the fish would probably have been lost. Ten minutes later Terry has single-handedly subdued the bluefin. When the boat returns to San Diego two days later, the tuna weighs in at three hundred and ninety-eight pounds, the largest Pacific bluefin tuna ever caught by man using any method.

There have been many remarkable achievements in the brief history of the tribe and they were accomplished by equally remarkable men. I would not want to put one above another, but here in the last hours of the tribe's existence it is most unlikely that Terry's feat will ever be surpassed. His bluefin belongs to the tribe. It is a symbol of the ultimate achievement for a hunter in the wilds of an unconquerable ocean.

In another time and place, this event would have been celebrated for weeks and brought great distinction to Terry and his people. The tale would have turned to legend and lived for as long as his clan existed. Here in the late twentieth century it passed unnoticed. But then the blue water hunter is not entirely of this century. Beneath the surface of the oceans, he has found a seam in time and has backtracked his way into an ancient wilderness. He brings little evidence of his century with him, he comes naked and alone, and for that reason he absorbs the natural world of the ocean as it absorbs him. It lives in him as the earth and its creatures once lived in the tribes of the land. To return is to be of it and during those moments in the ocean, when he has found the seam, an empty space is filled: he has returned inward to his natural home.

***

I'm as removed from those who hunt the tuna as I can be, yet still be in the same ocean. My thoughts are not on new territories to explore, but on the old ones that have disappeared, the rich untouched ocean that the fathers experienced fifty years ago. If I could find a seam in time, that is where I would go. Not to hunt, but to see and feel the teeming life that existed here on the island and along the coastline.

The bottom is thick with lobsters, many as long as your leg and as big around as a ball player's thigh. Spider crabs with four-foot leg spans wrestle in the sand for tasty morsels. Abalone big as dinner plates hang on every available rock, and scallops a foot across nudge one another into the cracks and crevices of a thousand untouched reefs along the coastline.

In the spring I'd swim off the beach and into the Laguna kelp beds and watch the schools of white sea bass drift through the kelp forests, walls and walls of them shimmering in the overhead light of a midday sun. The yellowtail, fifty and sixty-pounders in schools by the thousands, cruising the perimeter of the bed, shouldering their bulk through the outside strands, looking for bait fish that run in schools so thick that the light bouncing off their silver bodies blinds the eye. The sea is alive with free swimming bonito, barracuda, calico, and the sandy bottom carpeted with halibut come to spawn.

The stark emptiness of the sandy bottom jars me from my reverie and I stare into the naked cove where two fish, as white as the sand, watch me from below.

The days pass and the season is near for the Santa Ana winds that erupt suddenly and violently out of the east. This journey is near its end. I postpone the inevitable for a few more days, and then call Ernie. We shall be taking the *Infinity* back to Dana Point in six days.

My first thoughts are to prepare for my reentry into civilization, but a closer look shows there is really little to do. To prepare for events and situations that lie in the future is counter to the life I've been living. No, there is nothing to do. Whatever lies before me will be there until I'm upon it. The question that disturbs me is, to what home do I return? This cove, these fickle waters, the island, the sky, the birds of both land and sea, and the creatures of the ocean on whose roof the *Infinity* rests—this is home.

These last days fill me. I understand enough to know that this time and these events will not come again. This journey had the magic of the beginner's voyage and it will stay with me all my days. Knowing my time is short, I devour each hour, seeing all there is to see and hearing the sounds of the cove that have turned to a kind of soft music. The familiar scents of the ocean wash up on the small beach astern, and I close my eyes and inhale the pungent odors. Taking off my clothes, a pair of shorts, I let the warm wind of late summer run across me then dive naked into the cool ocean, my body charged with voltage from the sharp exchange.

***

The black ball of bait had moved into the cove while I was off making my phone call to Ernie. The birds were working it from the top when I returned. Later the school moved close to the *Infinity* for protection and the birds could only work the outside fringe of the fifty-foot ball. This is not a loosely packed school of anchovy like those that normally run along the outside kelp. This is a deep water school and they are packed solid, like a moving ink blot. These dense schools were around years ago, and I thought they had disappeared along with everything else. Seizing the moment, I jump into the water and shoot a roll of film using the tight structure of the school's form as a subject.

Later, in the last two hours of daylight, the predators begin to work the school—calicos, barracuda and the occasional bonito. Watching the water boil with fish is exciting and in their over-aggressiveness, the barracuda come straight out of the water in their pursuit of the bait and do full flips in midair before splashing back. On the aft deck of the *Infinity* I rig up a small lure and cast into the bait from the stern, catching several barracuda and a half dozen small calicos, then return them to the water. Night falls and the activity dies with the light. Sure that the bait will disappear during the night, I thank the provider for this final pleasure.

The following evening the bait make a surprise return and give me another evening's worth of brisk line fishing. I can look down from the stern into the clear water and see the calico and barracuda chase the lure right up to the boat, then turn away at the last instant before it breaches the surface. Again and again I throw the lure out and reel it in as fast as I can, trying to get the fish to hit it. Near dark I'm looking over the side, watching the fish chase the lure and swimming right under the hull of the *Infinity*, toward the bait, is a white sea bass! A big one. Had they not left the island over a month ago? Is this the supreme gift? The white, I know, will hang around the bait and feed on it. All I've got to do is slip into the water and mingle with the bait until the fish hits it. I should have an easy straight-on shot.

Not wanting to take the time to put on a wet suit, I enter the water with mask, fins, snorkel and my cocked speargun. The bait is twenty feet from the boat and I swim to its center. The tightly packed anchovies can't avoid me and I feel their tiny slick bodies brush against my skin. Several minutes pass. A barracuda runs into the school, begins to hit it, sees me three feet away and turns on a dime, zipping away in the opposite direction. I am eight feet under the water in the middle of the school when the thick body of bait opens before me like a yawn and I point the speargun in the direction of the gap as it widens. There, a hand's length away from the tip of my arrow, at point blank range, is the white sea bass. It freezes before me and our eyes meet. I do not pull the trigger.

"Fly away, spirit fish."

The white sea bass turns on itself and hurtles past the small reef and into the haze, out of sight.

"Run free, and live out your life, ocean warrior."

OTHER BOOKS BY CARLOS EYLES

Diving Free

Sea Shadows

The Blue Edge

Secret Seas

Dolphin Borne

AVAILABLE TITLES BY CARLOS EYLES

THE BLUE EDGE

In this near mystical journey, Carlos returns to the once bountiful Sea of Cortez he explored as a free diver over thirty years ago. Finding it lacking, he continues on to a distant archipelago, one rumored to hold great fish and sharks by the thousands, soaring manta rays, and breaching whales. Here on the ocean's edge, he tales the reader on breathhold dives into an extremely dangerous yet magical realm.

"A masterful story by Carlos Eyles who reveals in an absorbing tale the plight of the seas. Beautifully written with fascinating depictions of sea life. As important a book as Rachel Carson's The Sea Around Us".—**Clive Cussler, author**

360 pages, 5-1/2x8-1/5, paper..**$16.95**
ISBN 1-881652-27-0

SECRET SEAS

In this rich collection of 16 short stories and essays Eyles takes the reader to the far corners of the heart and mind, as well as the ocean's realm in Micronesia, California, the Sea of Cortez and the Bahamas. These stories of the sea and man's interaction with its creatures represent the search for meaning and spirituality in the alien environment from which we came.

"Eyles writes about a wilderness—the wilderness within each of us—as it is reflected back through the environment. He takes us beyond the safe confines of the unknown, like the free diver, unencumbered, vulnerable, operating in an alien environment with uncommon ease."—**Michael Menduno from the Foreword**

160 pages, 5-3/8x8-1/2, paper **$12.95**
ISBN 0-922769-23-0

DOLPHIN BORNE

Dolphin Borne is a sea survival story that develops into a message of the sea's creatures to mankind. When a veteran and a novice blue water hunter are stalking prey off an island in the Sea of Cortez, the novice spears a large amberjack that proves more than he can handle. The fish bolts for the open sea pulling the novice with it. When it finally tires, the hunter is caught in strong currents heading down the channel. The veteran comes to his assistance, and the two must survive by their skills and what little they have with them. Eyles weaves a masterly tale that twists and turns with the unexpected, where the impossible becomes possible and the real becomes surreal. It is a breathtaking adventure that ends with a series of phantasmagoric experiences that become only too real. Though a novel, this is a classic Carlos Eyles adventure you won't want to miss.

160 pages, 5-1/2x8-1/2, paper **$12.95**
ISBN 0-922769-25-7

DIVING FREE HAWAII

Carlos has established a free diving school in Kona, Hawaii called Diving Free Hawaii. It closely follows his philosophy of infusing the human elements of mind, body, and spirit with the ocean world thus allowing the diver to intimately interact with the environment. He offers three distinct levels of development: beginner, intermediate and advanced diver. Each level is designed to enable the free diver to reach his full potential in the water. More information is available through his website:

www.carloseyles.com